Gender-based violence

NEUE DENKANSÄTZE IN DEN BILDUNGS- UND SOZIALWISSENSCHAFTEN

NEW APPROACHES IN EDUCATIONAL AND SOCIAL SCIENCES

Herausgegeben von / Edited by Gerd-Bodo von Carlsburg,
Anne Kirschner, Natalija Mažeikienė

BAND/VOL. 43

Giuseppina Cersosimo (ed.)

Gender-based violence

Social implications for health

PETER LANG

Bruxelles - Berlin - Chennai - Lausanne - New York - Oxford

Library of Congress Cataloging-in-Publication Data
Names: Cersosimo, Giuseppina, editor.
Title: Gender based violence : social implications for health / Giuseppina Cersosimo.
Description: Brussels ; New York : Peter Lang, [2025] | Includes bibliographical references.
Identifiers: LCCN 2024044785
Subjects: LCSH: Gender-based violence. | Women--Violence against. | Girls--Violence against.
Classification: LCC HV6250.4.W65 G4648 2024 | DDC 363.32082--dc23/eng/20241127
LC record available at https://lccn.loc.gov/2024044785

Bibliographic Information published by the Deutsche Nationalbibliothek
The Deutsche Nationalbibliothek lists this publication in the Deutsche Nationalbibliografie; detailed bibliographic data is available in the internet at http://dnb.d-nb.de.

An electronic version of this book is freely available, courtesy of libraries collaborating with Knowledge Unlatched (KU). KU is a pioneering initiative aimed at making high-quality books Open Access for the public benefit. The Open Access ISBN for this book is 978-3-0343-5510-0. For more details and access to the OA version, visit www.knowledgeunlatched.org.

Cover illustration by Lucia Landolfi and Assunta Penna.

ISSN 1434-8748
ISBN 978-3-0343-5509-4 (Print)
E-ISBN 978-3-0343-5510-0 (E-PDF)
E-ISBN 978-3-0343-5511-7 (E-PUB)
DOI 10.3726/b22481

Published by Peter Lang Éditions Scientifiques Internationales - P.I.E.,
Brussels, Belgium
info@peterlang.com - www.peterlang.com

PETER LANG
open

This publication has been peer reviewed.

Contents

Giuseppina Cersosimo

Introduction. An interdisciplinary reading of gender-based violence

The central question of this volume is the violence against women and young girls as part of symbolic or systemic violence, overt or subtle, culminating in femicide, and its impact on their health and overall wellbeing.

Violence, recognized as a determinant of health, has been aptly described as a silent epidemic affecting women not only in Europe but globally. According to European Union statistics, one in three women aged fifteen and older has experienced physical or sexual violence, including instances of rape, murder, and brutality. These tragic occurrences, reported across Europe and beyond, have intensified discussions on strategies for preventing and combatting these crimes. Additionally, there is a growing recognition that violence against women not only exacts a heavy toll on mortality but also inflicts substantial physical and emotional suffering on entire communities.

The resistance to modernization processes, stemming from patriarchal traditions, has led to the persistent rejection of gender equality. This, in turn, underscores the limitations of the equality process, which objectively seeks to reestablish the primacy of male roles. Gender equality is not only a fundamental human right but also an essential condition for an all-inclusive democracy to which everyone can and should belong.

By safeguarding the rights of women and girls and enhancing their empowerment through equitable access to education, healthcare, decent employment, and effective representation in decision-making processes, we can foster sustainable economies, which will benefit societies and humanity.

Conceiving society as an advocate for victims of violence at all organizational levels, one that ensures the timely and effective prosecution of perpetrators, empowers survivors, and lends support to all those committed to assisting them. This, in turn, progressively discourages those who believed they could act with impunity.

This book aims to provide an additional platform for discussing the issue of violence against women and young girls, with a particular focus on its implications for health, employment, education, training, and life trajectories, all from the standpoint of equality.

Our comprehensive examination of the delays in combatting violence and its multifaceted effects suggests the adoption of multidisciplinary analytical and linguistic frameworks. These frameworks can foster concepts related to the prevention and combatting of violence, along with the development of practices and models that promote the well-being and health of women.

The contributors to this volume discuss the critical challenges facing women and girls around the world in terms of their freedom, autonomy and safety. The book examines discrimination, violence and health across the life course; environmental change and violence against women; symbolic and systemic violence; digital environments and new forms of violence; self-representation, languages and violence; young girls and violence; generations, violence and culture; territories and violence. The chapters draw on secondary and primary empirical sources on the future of women and girls, focussing on the health and well-being of their own futures.

The majority of chapters supplement their discussion with the survey and other data, while others draw on secondary sources and reviews of scholarship to discuss policy implications and ultimately improve the fight against violence against women and girls in transitional societies.

The book is divided into ten chapters.

In the first chapter, *gender-based violence: As a social determinant of health*, Giuseppina Cersosimo aims to explain how gender power relations are at the root of GBV and are among the most influential social determinants of health. The latter operate across many dimensions of life, affecting how people live, work and relate to each other, and whether women have a voice or degree of control over their lives and health.

In the second chapter, *Pathways of women's health and protection. A culturally sensitive approach against violence*, Sonia Viale and Maria Concetta Segneri, propose that Promoting the culture of violence prevention and defending the right to health from a culturally sensitive perspective means promoting women's awareness and broad access to health care pathways. The paper shows that the management of the relational and operational complexity involved in interventions to deal with situations of gender violence against foreign women and their children requires the identification of good professional practices. This work aims to contribute to the methodological reflection on the management of cases of gender violence against foreign women and girls, whether mothers or not, in the health sector.

In the third chapter, *From domination to care. Recognizing and combating the common root of gender violence and environmental degradation*, Daniela Belliti has highlighted the link between climate change and gender-based violence and as the phenomenon is fuelling the increase in migration flows, in which the female component is preponderant. These data seem to confirm the ecofeminist thesis (since its origin to the latter philosophical development) that there is a link between violence against women and violence against nature.

Continuing this line of research in the fourth chapter, *The great destruction: Violence against women, against the planet, against all life*, Maria Lucia Piga and Patrizia Desole explain that the environmental crisis and violence against women are among the crucial issues affecting contemporary society, both because of the violence they imply and because of the widening gap in inequalities. Although the two dimensions may seem distant and distinct (macro and micro, respectively), environmental degradation and violence against women are in fact two sides of the same coin, a sword of Damocles hanging over the whole of humanity and the survival of the planet and its biodiversity.

Also in chapter five, *Climate violence, gendered migration and women's health: What relationship and what protection?*, Angela di Stati and Anna Iermano focus on "climate violence" and show that efforts are being made at the international level to increase women's participation in the formulation and implementation of policies and action plans to respond to climate change and disasters, to reduce risks and to influence decisions in this regard.

In chapter six, *Epigenetics of violence against women: From molecular scars to precision prevention*, Simona Gaudi and Sara Mellano go beyond the relevance that gender-based violence continues to have in our daily lives and show that an innovative and intersectoral vision is needed to limit its physical and psychological consequences on women's health. The problem is complex and multifaceted, requiring the integration of molecular research with rigorous statistical analysis and with social, educational, clinical and care interventions.

In chapter seven, Taking care of those left behind: Social workers facing children involved into feminicide, Barbara Segatto and Valentina Amerighi, examine how social workers responsible for looking after children in vulnerable situations dealt with this specific case and what they felt they needed to work in the best interests of the children. the findings highlight the prevalence of deep trauma experienced by the social workers themselves and the lack of appropriate tools to achieve effective goals.

In chapter eight, *Analysis of femcel's online experiences: Internalised violence?*, Assunta Penna and Debora Maria Pizzimenti investigate how in ubiquitous digital environments, hate speech is particularly visible and widespread: sexist comments and threats, racist insults and homophobic attacks find an ideal space to express themselves online. In general, women are the main targets of online hate speech. Using digital media ethnography, the researchers examined the Femcel discussion platform known as "Crystalcafe" to explore how patriarchy, internalized misogyny and lookism interact and shape the experiences of its users.

To follow in chapter 9, *Misgendering and transgender women: Between minority stress, resistance and embedded imaginaries,* Giuseppe Masullo and Marianna Coppola highlight the need to examine violence as a phenomenon not limited to women, but extending to all those categories of people (including transgender and/or non-binary people, etc.) who are discriminated against, oppressed and marginalized because of their gender identity and expression. Drawing on a study conducted with a sample of transgender women, the essay shows how digital environments are proving to be useful contexts for the performance of chosen gender, but also environments in which old and new forms of oppression are evident.

At the end of chapter ten, *Violence against older women in Italy: Understanding the scope and possible interventions* Stefano Poli, Paola Giannoni, and Giada Moretti aim to provide new evidence on violence against older women in Italy by presenting a survey carried out in Genoa, a metropolitan urban context characterized by a significant demographic ageing, investigating episodes of suffered violence and/or discrimination on a sample of 1,354 residents over 65 living in the community.

At the end of my brief introductory remarks, allow me to remind you that, since the 2011 Instanbul Convention, one of the recognized actions has been the elimination of all forms of violence against women, but the proclamation of a right does not correspond to its realization and does not even guarantee that the right proclaimed is valid once and for all: it could be called into question, modifying its grounds and objectives, explicitly or implicitly, but as long as we have rules, we must remember that they are a point of reference for the reality and actions of individuals. The premise for the construction of a health, well-being, social security that should guarantee to everyone, regardless of their location and the inequalities they bear, the positive results of their right not to be violated or owned by others. This is not something to be taken for granted or taken for granted, but something to be maintained every day as a premise of a democratic society.

Giuseppina Cersosimo

Gender-based violence:
As a social determinant of health

Abstract: This chapter shows that gender-based violence (GBV) is internationally recognized as a serious and pervasive phenomenon that affects the lives and health of girls
and women.

The World Health Organization (WHO) reports that around 30 % of women worldwide
have experienced some form of violence. In addition to the obvious immediate effects, GBV
has long-term consequences, including increased incidence of many non-communicable
diseases such as diabetes and cancer. This paper aims to explain how gender power relations
are at the root of GBV and are among the most influential social determinants of health.
They operate across many dimensions of life, affecting how people live, work and relate to
each other, and whether women have a voice or degree of control over their lives and health.

Premise

Violence against women has a specificity that does not allow it to be assimi-
lated with other apparently similar manifestations: it is inextricably linked to the
modalities of the relationship between the public and the private spheres, and
between men and women in both spheres, with their respective roles. In fact,
relations between the two sexes have historically involved not only differential
access to socially relevant resources (prestige, power and wealth), but also the
personal dependence of women on men and the subordination of the female
body to male power. These phases of violence are the result of a question of identity and its recognition, as well as that of new roles for women: it is therefore
essential to explain violence in university classrooms and at all levels of school-
ing, in order to teach how to recognize it as a cultural and social legacy that the
Western and civilized world must confront and put an end to.

In fact, formal equality between men and women, although enshrined in law,
does not yet correspond to substantive equality in areas where power is exercised, such as politics, work, the economy and finance: here women are fewer
and mostly in subordinate roles.

This is the result of an identity-related issue linked to identification and
new perspectives for women. The repetition of brutal violent acts against
women should be explained in its historical context. Two variables should be

considered: personal identity in men and women which is not acquired once and for all but is linked to times, roles and society; and power not as a physical force, but as an ensemble of expressive features transferred to identity and socio-economic status.

The extent to which this concentration of power has devastated the female presence over time has been the subject of long narratives. Here it is only appropriate to reiterate that power has its own history and its own tradition, the importance of which cannot be forgotten, and is a determining part of daily life.

Simmel had already pointed at some hints concerning social issues as he said: "If the relation between sexes is taken to its extreme, i.e. to the master-slave relation, the master has the privilege not to be forced to repeat continually that he is the master. Instead, the slave cannot forget it. It should be recognized that women are more likely to forget that they are women rather than a man would forget that he is a man" (Simmel, 1996, p. 92).

Indeed, the forms of "not forgetting" are many, because "every physical difference is characterised by a universal and immutable aspect", in fact "gender is one of the recurrent references with which political power has been conceived, legitimized and criticized. It concerns, but at the same time determines, the meaning of the opposition between male and female. ... In this way, the binary opposition and the social process of gender relations become part of the meaning of power itself: to question or change one of these aspects is to jeopardise the whole system" (Scott, 2013, p. 39 e 61).

Giddens (1992) too explains the nexus between modern male violence and female sexual freedom by saying that women no longer accept sexual predominance and both sexes have to deal with this new perspective. And he continues by saying that a large part of male violence is triggered by disorientation and inadequacy. Violence is the destructive reaction to the decline of female complicity.

It should be added that in his "language" violence, violation, become a memory imprinted on a body: from a slap to rape, they become an unspeakable memory that combines oppression and humiliation, the first result of which, as many who deal with the problem know, is the reluctance to narrate it, a lexicon that overwhelms any other language.

The principles of freedom, personal autonomy and equality remained dangerously confused in the private sphere with the ideals of complementarity. The idea that a woman's life should be devoted to caring for her family and her husband has legitimized unbridled attacks on the practice of submission that this destiny entails. However, this has gradually been undermined by a transformation of fundamental rights, which were originally based on the idea of equality regardless of differences between individuals (gender, race, language, religion, social condition, etc.) and have increasingly been called upon to deal with differences.

In this case, the issue of culture is clearly re-emerging, since the vulnerability and subordination of the female body, which was explicitly sanctioned in the past by legal norms, cultures and social practices, is still implicitly reaffirmed today, not only by the sexism of the dominant culture, often supported by other women, but also by the endless trail of violence that runs through the lives of women of different classes and territorial origins.

And if modernity has placed personal freedoms at the heart of social relations, it has also more or less implicitly foreseen or tolerated that women have fewer rights in terms of freedom over their own bodies and less social and legal recognition of work care at home

In other words, despite the affirmation of fundamental rights, it seems that Kofi Annan, then President of the United Nations, rightly said that violence against women is likely to be the most outrageous form of breach of fundamental rights. Violence against women knows neither boundaries nor culture nor richness. Until we stop it, we won't be able to say that we have achieved real progress towards equality, development and peace (Kofi Annan, 1999); this is apparently not fully understood even in the most modern and advanced Western societies.

It is clear that even legal societies cannot escape cultural legacies and the social relations that are often an integral part of them. Women must be protected, but this protection must be built together with others, with others, it cannot be left to the legislator alone: it is the restoration of control, which seemed to have disappeared, by these communities. Awareness-raising against violence must therefore be seen as a comparison to complete the path of citizenship rights, with the constant commitment of women and men. This fight must be waged at several levels, involving the processes of socialization and the construction of sexual identities, culture and education, laws and their means of implementation, professions and institutions, the organization of work and everyday family life. The principle on which we should try to reason is education in feelings, respect for others, diversity, because we are what we are thanks to others and our relationships with them, on a path that must include, also through memory, the youngest and the youngest. Identity is a social construction and we build ourselves thanks to others, thanks to the diversity that others represent for us.

Contributing to the fight against violence against women would mean giving them the freedom to live without the fear and stress of having to defend themselves against violent men, their partners, husbands, acquaintances and work colleagues. It would also mean that the social determinants of health, which depend on gender and violence, could be variables on which to work, together with the culture of acceptance and respect for differences, in order to limit public and social health costs and restore women's well-being and health.

Reflecting on gender and violence as social determinants of health

It is important to explain why gender and violence are social determinants of health. Gender and violence are two social characteristics that have a direct impact on the health status of the population, with crucial implications for the social context and the "determinants of health" or "social determinants of health" (Marmot, 2006; Rodgers, 2002). The concept of social determinants of health refers to the relationship between social position and the cause of disease, an important factor in the study of health. Those who live in a violent environment have a greater risk of contracting a variety of pathologies (from fractures to gastrointestinal problems, from wounds and burns to psychiatric problems, etc.) and a greater need to access and use health services to restore their health.

Moreover, these factors, which are interrelated but also heterogeneous, if not randomly distributed, cause inequalities in health and well-being. Finally, and this is an unfortunate reality, it has been historically proven that the deterioration of the environment and quality of life is often accompanied by indifference, arrogance and violence in relationships, a process that affects women and minors in particular.

Too often, violence has not received the necessary and non-deferrable attention and intervention, and common sense has prevented a timely and appropriate response. Over time, however, violence against women's bodies has generated progressive and ambivalent social dissent. In particular, the Istanbul Convention (2011) has brought unprecedented attention to the social and biological health impacts of violent behaviour on women. From femicide to beatings, stalking and the use of force, violence in its various forms, explicit and implicit, symbolic and systemic, visible and invisible, has too often remained a dramatic and in many cases unchallenged expression of power on the part of the stronger, because it is recognized as such at a biological level or because of legislation that is sometimes interpreted in a way that is still patriarchal and socially punitive for women. The power of violence causes general, bodily and identity damage, violating physical integrity, but also symbolic, humiliating and marginalizing, with obvious family and social repercussions, for example on children. The two bodies, the social one, expressed in everyday life, and the biological one, directly attributable to women's historical functions, are a unique place for the manifestation of this violence, an offence that combines damage to the body and person of women. The social body and the biological body cannot be separated from their unified expression, the articulation of a culture in which social and environmental relations have already modified and will continue to modify, today and tomorrow, the existence and the consequent pathologies of women. Violence, present in all societies, is a social phenomenon that spans several eras, albeit with specific characteristics at each time. The WHO report (2021) stresses that violence against women is "a health problem of enormous global proportions", in a situation aggravated by environmental changes, with significant short, medium and long-term consequences for women's health and well-being (Cersosimo, 2019; 2023). What can be defined as "the habit of violence", which sometimes becomes common sense without being noticed, makes us lose sight of the deterioration in health that it represents, both in general (a disease that looms) and in its effects (a disease that spreads). This is also because there is a growing awareness that violence, in its current form and its potential, has serious repercussions, not only in terms of mortality, but also in terms of considerable physical and emotional suffering for women. Violence thus becomes a (proximal) social determinant of health, which not only causes public health problems (Garcia-Moreno et al., 2005) due to the wounds or even mutilations inflicted on the bodies of many women, but can also determine the onset of pathologies ranging from the most well-known depression to gastric pathologies, neoplasms and infectious diseases (sexually transmitted).

Conclusions. Finding new synergies between knowledge

Violence against women is a major public health problem and a violation of human rights. It has short and long-term negative effects on the physical, mental, sexual and reproductive health of the victim, often causing a crisis of self-esteem which has the immediate effect of shattering one's identity, isolating and paradoxically seeking isolation, fearing the judgement of others, inability to work like others, reduced ability to take care of oneself and one's children. It is one's own role as such that is questioned in a constant anxiety, in the face of the fear of what one did not think could happen: "People are afraid when misfortune strikes them suddenly. They are overwhelmed by fear when something completely unfamiliar comes their way" (Sofsky, 2005, p. 27).

Moreover, those who look at violence from the outside often try to understand that "anxiety" is a state that pervades the whole person. It conditions his sensations, colours his perceptions, slows down his actions, rests like a nightmare on his life. Even when the cue is forgotten, it continues to keep the individual in a state of agitated vigilance. Nothing is certain. Eventually, the anxiety becomes entrenched in the person's behaviour: "discouragement and fear become characteristic" (Sofsky 2005, p. 28).

But this factor of violence leads to another question: to what extent is it possible to accept indifference to the pain of others, and how can we educate ourselves, better educate ourselves, to perceive it, to recognize it, to make it part of our secondary socialization?

In some cases it seems that this violence, which does not exist in the empyrean but is always constructed in relations, becoming an image, a language, a bodily expression, a silence, an aggression, an isolation, acquires a charm, expresses a power more powerful than other powers, certainly capable of superior dynamics and execution, faster than those of democracy. And the fewer weapons it has, the stronger it will be felt: one could even say of its seductive ambivalence, like those hands that can caress and then destroy and then caress again, causing pain and suffering.

Wolfgang Sofsky, in his classic essay on violence, reminds us that "the weapons of violence are not only stones, iron, dust or machines: they are also the ability to use them, the knowledge and skill, the cunning and malice of men. Only the human gesture frees the weapon from a potential state and makes it what it is, an instrument of destruction (Sofsky, 1996).

The transition from human to non-human expresses this path, if, as Simone Weil said, to do evil (hence "to do wrong") is to reduce man (being) to a thing.

In this debate probably the old Weil's quotation best exemplifies the indisputably dehumanizing role of violence: "Nothing has the power to interpose between its impulse and act. ...Thus the violence obliterates anybody who feels its touch. It comes to seem just as external to its employer as to its victim. And from these springs the idea of a destiny before which executioner and victim stand equally innocent, before which conquered and conqueror are brothers in the same distress" (Weil, 1965, p. 17). There is an element here that we must bear in mind and that seems to break the democracy with which we collect violence: several authors agree that there is a suffering that goes beyond being elaborated, as Franco Rella says, a suffering that goes beyond the image, the language, the word. A suffering that can never be understood or communicated, that therefore never becomes an experience and that seems condemned to an inexorable dissolution; here the pain is expressed in all its immediacy, without the mediation of articulated language.

All this also has an impact on girls and boys who witness violence in the family, who are themselves invisible and in most cases silent victims of this situation, and who can suffer from emotional and behavioural disorders. The effects of gender-based violence affect the well-being of the entire community, exacerbating the direct and indirect costs to public health and society as a whole. For example, not only hospitalization in the most violent cases, but also absenteeism from work due to illness and the inability to manage daily routines with children and/or elderly parents.

Violence against women affects the whole world, as we said, but the latest available data comparing rates of gender-based violence in Europe is from 2018. The next cross-national report will not be published at the end 2024. Furthermore, some countries do not include gender-based violence in their statistics. This prompted the European Data Journalism Network and the Mediterranean Institute for Investigative Reporting to manually collect their data from 20 EU countries. In Greece, Slovenia, Germany and Italy, the number of feminicides is on the rise: "Since 2019, MIIR journalist Janine Louloudi explained that countries such as Greece, Slovenia, Germany and Italy have seen a significant increase in feminicides. Greece recorded the highest increase in feminicides in 2021, with a peak of 187.5 %, from 8 in 2020 to 23 in 2021." It is also important to bear in mind that, according to experts, this is linked to the control that men exercised over women in the home during the pandemic. Control that was lost when restrictions were lifted. And this may be why we saw a radical increase in violence against women in the first year of the pandemic and then a spike in femicides in 2021 in some countries.

This violent power is often exercised by husbands, friends, acquaintances, etc. When violence is perpetrated by strangers, it implies a persistent orientation towards the female body as a body to be violated and insulted, for sexual purposes, punishment or revenge, and the freedom of women to dispose of their own bodies, the space in which they live and relate to others, is more limited than that of men. When violence occurs between close relatives or blood relatives, it obviously stems from the perception of a transgression: that is, the factors just mentioned, which are obviously part of the commands and indications of the respective men and part of the women, are violated, explicitly or latently, in the perception that the subject tends to acquire an autonomous role and behaviour (Collins, 2013), more attentive to an external dimension than to the internal and traditional one of relationships.

Even the feeling that women can live in mutually antagonistic contexts, starting from the emergence of new languages and meanings, perceptions and desires, encourages male behaviour aimed at "withdrawing" from these orientations and experiences, using the language of violence as the lowest common denominator. This is an issue that, for many reasons, is not discussed by any of the participants, thus excluding it as a factor in the process, but how can we fail to remember that "the changes in power between women and men are central to the decline in fertility, even if this is rarely recognised" (MacKinnon, 1997, p. XI). It is therefore an undeniable, though often unspoken, contributor to the demographic transition, in fact the process of reproduction is one of the first to be questioned as a female "role" with the emergence of any new professionalism and solidarity.

To paraphrase Nelson Mandela in the foreword to the World report on violence and health, it is important to remember that health, like security, "is not achieved as if by chance, but is the result of collective consensus and public investment" (Mandela, 2002, p. V). It is therefore necessary to rethink how knowledge can contribute to processes that allow us to trace, classify and monitor the lives of women who have suffered violence, in order to understand pathologies, ways, times and spaces for new protections and readjustments of the self and the reconstruction and affirmation of one's own identity. An interdisciplinary scientific approach to the effects of violence can, for example, implement good practices to achieve better awareness through specific courses in medical faculties and health professions degree courses, develop communication models, monitoring and social antennas to build forms and methods of assistance, health and otherwise, privileged for women and their children. This process can counteract any form of stigmatization and promote and guarantee the right to health in the short, medium and long term.

References

Carsosimo, G. (2023). *Salute e benessere delle donne. Ambiente Disuguaglianze e Violenza*. Liguori, Napoli.

Cersosimo, G. (2019). Double-Edged intimate relationships. When violence has a complicity between victim and executioner. *BUT- Series VII Social Sciences. Law, 12*(61), No. 1, 111–126. https://doi.org/10.31926/but.ssl.2019.12.61.1.11

Collins, R. (2013). Entering and leaving the tunnel of violence: Micro-sociological dynamics of emotional entrainment in violent interactions. *Current Sociology, 61*(2), 132–151. https://doi.org/10.1177/0011392112456500

Garcia-Moreno, C., Heise, L., Jansen, H. A., Ellsberg, M., & Watts, C. (2005). Public health. Violence against women. *Science, 25*;310(5752), 1282–1283. doi: 10.1126/science.1121400. PMID: 16311321.

Giddens, A. (1992). *The transformation of intimacy: Sexuality, love and eroticism in modern societies*. Cambridge: Polity.

Hilbert, M. (2013). Technological information inequality as an incessant moving target: The redistribution of information and communication capacities between 1986 and 2010. *Journal of the American Society for Information Science and Technology*, 65(4), 821–835.

Kofi, A. A. (1999). Violence against women. Retrieved from https://www.un.org/womenwatch/daw/followup/session/presskit/fs4.htm.

Mandela N. (2002). Foreword World Health Organization. (2002). World report on violence and health: Summary. World Health Organization. https://iris.who.int/handle/10665/42512, p.v.

MacKinnon, A. (1997). *Love and freedom. Professional women and the reshaping of personal life*. Cambridge: Cambridge University Press.

Marmot, M. (2006). Status syndrome. A challenge to medicine. *Journal of the American Medical Association, JAMA*, 295(11), 1304–1307.

Rodgers, G. B. (2002). Income and inequality as determinants of mortality: An international cross-section analysis. *International Journal of Epidemiology, 31*, 533–538.

Scott, J. (2013). *Il "genere": un'utile categoria di analisi storica*. In I. Fazio (a cura di) J. Scott *Genere, politica, storia* (pp. 31–64). Roma: Viella.

Simmel, G. (1966). *Das Relative und das Absolute im Geschlechter-Problem*. Frankfurt am Main: Suhrkamp Verlag.

Sofsky, W. (1996). *Traktat über die Gewalt*. Frankfurt am Main: Fischer.

Sofsky, W. (2005). Rischio e Sicurezza. Torino: Giulio Einaudi.

Weil, S. (1965). *The Iliad, or the Poem of Force*. *Chicago Review, 18*(2), 5–30.

Sonia Viale and Maria Concetta Segneri

Women's health and protection paths. A culturally sensitive approach against violence

Abstract: Promoting the culture of violence prevention and the defense of the right to health from a culturally sensitive perspective means promoting women's awareness and broad access to healthcare pathways. The migratory experience amplifies isolation, barriers to access to services and conditions of lack of protection, forcing social and health workers to increase attention and expertise regarding reception and care practices.

The contribution of Psychology and Anthropology in this area is focussed on developing intervention models to combat inequalities in the field of health and making access easier for target populations who encounter greater critical issues.

The management of the relational and operational complexity, connected to interventions to take charge of situations of gender violence against foreign women and their children, requires the identification of good professional practices. Within the INMP clinic, differentiated protocols and health paths developed for the emergence and care of women victims of gender violence (domestic violence, trafficking and exploitation for sexual purposes). They designed to promote awareness of the violence suffered, the identification of needs and resources, health literacy, guidance in accessing social welfare services and legal protection.

This work intends to contribute to the methodological reflection on the management of cases of gender violence against foreign women and girls, whether mothers or not, in the healthcare sector.

Health intervention and women who have suffered violence

By their nature and the role they play in the family and in society, differently but transversally in all cultures, women are the subjects who suffer the most from the consequences of the changes and carry the burden of creating and maintaining balances too often precarious and dysfunctional. To help women to find, recognize and activate in themselves the abilities to face the state of confusion and disorientation in which they often find themselves because of the loss of points of reference and, consequently, of identity following the violence suffered, it allows us to work towards the emergence of a phenomenon of such magnitude as to involve the entire society.

An activity focussed on the prevention of discomfort and the protection of women's rights, in particular the right to health, is an intervention to promote the health of the family and the whole community.

The experience of INMP in the health and social care of foreign women has shown that gender-based violence is widespread in private contexts, in migration routes, based on discrimination that all too often women, as women, mothers, migrants, forced to the margins, segregated, in some cases trafficked. The physical and emotional reactions that accompany stories of ordinary violence, lived in silence and sometimes not recognized, confront women with the need to face very high levels of stress and manage very complex situations.

The healthcare context is the place where every demand for health, explicit, urgent and emerging needs are collected (WHO, 2014). In this context, offering a space for welcoming and caring for women who suffer violence is a challenge and a necessity. It is therefore crucial to facilitate access for those women for whom linguistic, cultural, economic and regulatory barriers are the greatest.

The aim is to provide women, through treatment and prevention, with the means to acquire the awareness and the possibility of recognition of their rights, also the right to fragility and to be able to ask for help. Synergy and network interventions between institutions and territorial realities dedicated to the protection of women help to contain and prevent the social costs of the multidimensional discomfort caused by violence.

Attention to listening and respect for differences are fundamental in order to create stronger relationships and remove as many barriers as possible, in favour of population groups approaching health and social and health services with greater difficulties and consequent discontinuity. They also play an important role in combating health inequalities by promoting the language and culture of prevention.

Different professional skills must come together to ensure an adequate response to the different demands of physical, mental, accompanying, supporting and monitoring health.

It is important to provide high-quality, uniform healthcare for all women, while helping them to formulate goals and a path out of violence based on the peculiarities and possibilities of each. It is equally important to return a reading of the violence suffered and the possibilities of emancipation in a language and in a manner consonant with the culture of belonging to foreign women, for which each intervention requires attention to the specificities related to the cultural context of origin. All this is possible by recognizing the difficulties of women themselves in acquiring full awareness of the violence suffered, due to past experiences of gender-based violence, in the context of origin and migration, causes of marginalization and social vulnerability. It is necessary to recognize forms of secondary victimization, due to intervention practices that reproduce different forms of violence based on structural barriers and understanding of differences.

The health paths

Clinical courses are "management tools" used by healthcare providers to define the best sequence of interventions aimed at patients with particular conditions or who may require specific procedures. The guiding principles that must guide the drafting of paths are the focus on the needs of the patient, multidisciplinarity, maximization of efficiency, the reduction of variations in clinical practice through the clarification of the sequence of acts of the professionals involved in the different phases: who must do, what must do, and when must do. The European Pathway Association, speaking of "care path" offers a complex definition: *A care path is a complex intervention, decision and organizational, of the care processes of a well-defined group of patients, during a well-defined period with the aim of improving the quality of care, promoting patient safety, optimising the use of resources* (Vanhaecht et al., 2007).

In the United Kingdom, "integrated care pathways" introduced in the early 1990s to increase system efficiency while maintaining or improving the quality of care, and to promote the development of the Evidence Base Medicine and the adoption of guidelines in daily practice, through the possibility of monitoring by process and outcome indicators (Cambell et al., 1998)

Social medicine must increase its skills and possibilities. The whole of society is calling for this, in order to guarantee the right to health for all, without neglecting the most disadvantaged sections of the population. It is also an ethical duty at the organizational level.

A health path aimed at managing the needs related to women who have suffered gender-based violence must be a concrete and feasible tool for the protection and promotion of vulnerable people, which counteracts inequalities in access/use to health services and services. The particularity of this management requires that it is entrusted to a multidisciplinary team with a specific preparation to the issues and gender language, dedicated to ensuring proper management of trauma from violence and assess the risk of re-victimization, also through, where possible, a socio-environmental investigation.

In cases where an immigrant woman has been subjected to violence, the presence of a transcultural mediator specialized in the health sector is important. Among the members of the multidisciplinary team, the cultural mediator brings into the setting linguistic, communicative skills, the mastery of non-verbal registers and variations in gender oriented communication registers, relational skills and regulatory and network skills.

The National Guidelines for Health Care Companies and Hospital Companies are currently in force in Italy on the subject of rescue and socio-health care for women victims of violence (DPCM 24 November 2017), which describe the path to be used in the emergency/emergency area but which does not have the same declination in non-emergency healthcare contexts. There is, therefore, a lack of attention to activities of early recognition of situations of gender-based violence if not related to physical symptoms that require emergency health access.

The "culturally sensitive" health path of the INMP

The health path for the management of women who suffer or have suffered gender-based violence within the polyclinic of the National Institute for the Promotion of the Health of Migrant Populations and the Fight against Diseases of Poverty (INMP) was designed to respond adequately to the health needs of women, as well as to encourage the emergence of all forms of gender-based violence and women's awareness of the violence suffered, identifying together with them the resources, inform them about their health rights, help them in access to social welfare services and legal protection. Through a targeted approach to the reception of fragility and the taking charge of the multidimensionality of discomfort, the health path provides personalized treatment and health promotion, multidisciplinary and synergistic. Moreover, in full respect of every woman, of differences and otherness in all its forms, it has been conceived with the aim of giving strength to the right to health, not only physical or psychological, nor merely understood as the absence of pathology, focussing on the personal, socio-cultural and environmental factors that women carry with them, beyond and despite the mechanisms of the violence suffered that, by their nature, tend to annihilate the will and right to exist.

It is preferred to speak of "health path" rather than "path of care" or "path of care", to highlight the active role of women themselves and to mark the value of empowerment (Zimmerman, 2000) which should be underpinned by any health and social-health intervention.

It speaks of "culturally sensitive path", wanting to understand the attention to variations according to the origin of the woman, so as to respect the cultural specificities, in particular of women on a migration path and second-generation immigrant women, who require dedicated attention to their family background and cultural background (Napier et al., 2014).

The staff of the INMP polyclinic consists of a multiprofessional staff of about 30 people, including doctors, nurses, OS, transcultural mediators, psychologists, anthropologists. The staff takes a transdisciplinary approach and an integrated approach to care. Applying the prefix

«trans» clearly shows the crossings, interdependencies, intersections, the mutual influence of individual and collective behaviours, and the spaces in «between». Overcoming polar positions in the face of the complexity of the existing. [...] Transculturality embraces hybridization. It is proposed to be reflected in the other without being so, but from this reflection comes transformed (whether it is individuals or society). It is the intrinsic potential of welcoming the other as the transformed self. (Reichardt, 2020: 150)

This method of health intervention based on the assumption that in order to meet a need for health it is necessary to consider its etiology, even implicit. In this regard, reference made to all health determinants, from social to economic (Gilmore et al., 2023).

The transdisciplinary approach that is the basis of the INMP intervention methodology refers to the concepts of "hybridization" and "cross-breeding" included in the reflections of Welsch (2001) and Moro et al. (2009), which the Institute joined.

Transculturality is establishing itself not only at the macrocultural level, but also at the individual level. For most of us, multiple cultural connections are decisive in terms of cultural education. We are cultural hybrids. [...] The work on one's own identity becomes more and more a work of integration of components of different cultural origin. And only the ability to cross transculturally will guarantee us identity and competence in the long run. (Welsch, 2001: 71, 73)

Adopting the expression "culturally sensitive" to define the health path for the management of women who have suffered gender-based violence produced by INMP reflects the need to adhere to a terminology easily traceable to the specific focus that the intervention aims at, or: taking care also of the socio-cultural diversity of the subjects to whom the intervention is directed.

Intercultural communication in the health field has not only to do with the topic of linguistic translation, but also with the understanding of concepts and practices related to the causes of diseases, different local views on what constitutes an effective health care service, and attitudes regarding acting and support. It must also be concerned with understanding the significance of different care communities and their role in improving access to expensive services, and containing any abuse. [...] In its best form, cultural competence thus bridges the cultural gap between "providers" and "consumers" of health care through an emphasis on the knowledge, attitudes and new skills of doctors. Competence concerns the creation and development of meaningful relationships. (Napier et al., 2014: 9)

The working group of the INMP that designed this health path has kept in mind the limits connected to this terminology, well reported by Napier et al. (2014: 10) when reporting the criticism made to the DSM (Diagnostic and Statistical Manual of Mental Disorders, A.P.A.) not to recognize their own cultural orientation and to maintain a unique point of view on the causes and meanings of mental suffering, taking inspiration from the new version of the "cultural formulation" of Bloomsbury contained in the DSM-V, aimed at providing mental health professionals with the tools to assess the potential effects of cultural factors on the development of mental illness.

Maintaining constant attention to these limits has been possible thanks to the inclusion of anthropologists and transcultural mediators in the design process of the healthcare intervention. In addition, this has allowed us to detail the ways in which subjective experiences differ from individual to individual not only in terms of meanings and interpretations given to words, expressions, practices, relationships, emotions, but also to biographical experiences, migration and multicultural meetings.

In the design of the culturally sensitive healthcare pathway for the management of gender-based violence cases, the INMP working group has first of all, taking into account the National Guidelines of Guidance and Guidance for Healthcare Companies and Hospital Companies in terms of assistance and socio-health to women victims of violence for health care companies and by hospitals that have an Emergency Room (Figure 1):

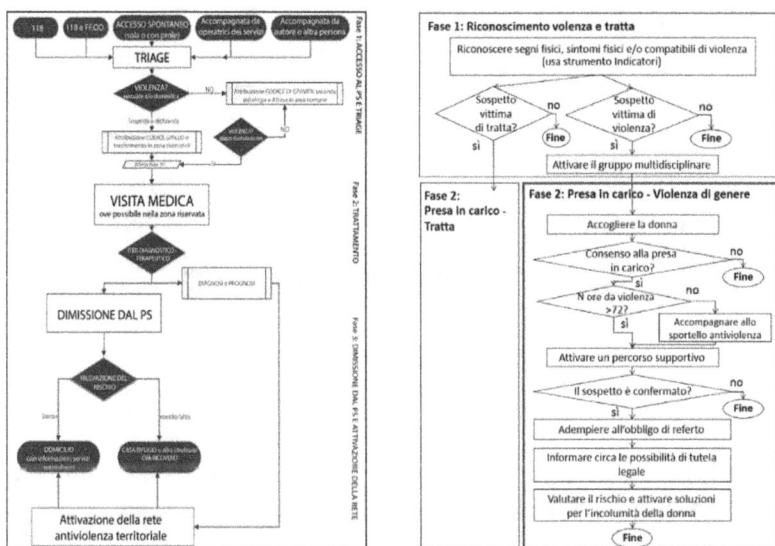

Figure 1. Health Trail Emergence Gender Violence PS VS INMP Health Path

In particular, it considered regulatory references, the use of indicators, the choice of tests, and the taking-over process. Subsequently, the working group tried to understand if the indicators and tools suggested were also suitable to bring out conditions of violence, and possible repetitions, when applied to foreign women. It is important, for example, to inform that, even in the event of a lack of a proper residence permit, women who are victims of violence have equal opportunities for protection.

Compared to existing instruments, verification with foreign women led to a revision of the material. Based on the experience gained, the working group identified some elements to be included in the assessment procedure present in the healthcare path, which could serve as calibrators of the weight given to indicators and tests. Among them are: the type of residence permit the woman was in possession of, the type of migration carried out to arrive in Italy, the current conditions of the housing and relational context. The inclusion of these three elements within the procedure allowed, in fact, to investigate previous conditions, experiences, and perceptions of women that could induce health workers or social-health workers to overestimate, or underestimate, a possible condition of violence reported by the woman during the assessment phase.

The three elements mentioned above have been identified because they represent easily accessible information in a health context, for example, the health card is the exclusive competence of those who have a residence permit. In addition, the request for the same elements may be little suspect by any accompanying persons to control the woman who arrived at the health services. These elements allow the emergence of women's experiences that can become signals for the proper management of tools such as, for example, having lived a negative migration experience could lead women to underestimate a possible risk of re-victimization having had in the past experiences of unprecedented violence (Figure 2).

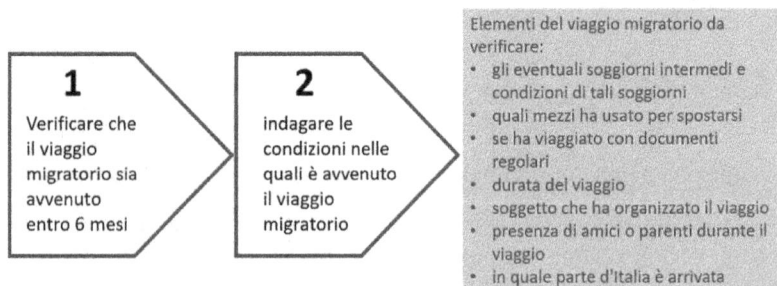

Figure 2. Investigating negative migration experience

Furthermore, living in conditions of housing promiscuity at the time of access to health services could easily expose women to assaults or other violence. Having arrived in Italy recently and not being able to count on an adequate territorial reference network is not a direct consequence of conditions of violence, but a contextual condition of recent arrival.

With regard to the risk of re-victimization, it is important to point out that in order to activate the protection solutions that are most appropriate to the needs of the individual woman, it is appropriate to collect information to understand whether the violence is recurrent (Figure 3).

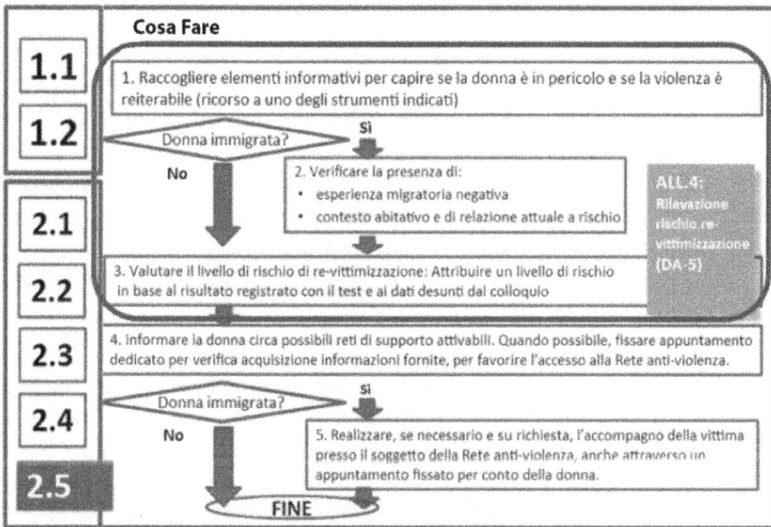

Figure 3. Assessing the risk of victimization of immigrant women

In conclusion, questioning these three elements during the procedure has strengthened the instruments of emergence of current or possible conditions of violence, personalizing the intervention from a brief and timely focus on the recent biographical experience of women. Brevity and speed are conditioning aspects of medical intervention, especially in very delicate cases such as gender violence. Therefore, changing health practices always involves a focus on the risk of adding tools that take too long to administer. The possibility of having an experienced, specialized and multi-professional working group in the case of the INMP has facilitated the process of reviewing the existing instruments, to identify small measures that could be significant in the presence of users of foreign origin.

The culturally sensitive health path for the management of women who suffer or have suffered gender-based violence of INMP should not be considered a standard procedure, but a trace adaptable to different healthcare, outpatient and counselling contexts, first and second level, and to the health workers present. The activities are developed through specialist medical visits, interviews for guidance and needs analysis, awareness raising, counselling, support, therapeutic paths of re-elaboration of trauma suffered. Each step of the health path provides for the acquisition of the free consent of women, without which the operator is not allowed to take any further action. In any case, the operator is asked to refrain from any judgment, making himself available in case of doubts or need for comparison, even in the future. It is important to promote the self-determination of women in full respect of their wishes, without any kind of coercion, ensuring all possible professional help.

The final goal of the path is to help women to get out of violence definitively through the construction of a relationship of help and interventions of health education, psychological empowerment and sending to the territorial anti-violence network. The multidisciplinary team is composed of nurses, transcultural mediators, psychologists and psychotherapists, gynecologists, infectious patients, anthropologists, social workers and lawyers, making use of moments of confrontation and interaction on cases. The working group is committed to enhancing personal resources, strengths, and at the same time to recognize fragility, prevent and reduce the onset of disorders related to experiences of loss, isolation or violence. This allows to better understand who comes to ask a question for help, the different meanings and the underlying reasons, helping the women themselves to bring out and explain a request for help sometimes too complex to clarify, in full respect, as well as the needs, the fundamental rights of the individual, in particular the right to health protection.

In case the woman is not Italian, before checking the above mentioned elements, it is necessary to calibrate the right distance between the subjects, which takes into account the socio-cultural differences as well as the individual sensitivity.

It is extremely important to assess the level of risk of re-victimization in order to inform women also about the possible support networks that can be activated, taking care to fix, to the need, a dedicated appointment to verify the acquisition of information by the woman and to support her in the phase of access to the anti-violence network (Figure 3).

Seeing things more closely, listening and welcoming, giving meaning to broken threads in the course of life: in this the intervention of the health worker becomes central and highlights aspects otherwise difficult to understand, useful to identify objectives and apply strategies of intervention as calibrated, effective as extremely respectful of both the uniqueness and belonging.

References

Campbell, H., Hotchkiss, R., Bradshaw, N., & Porteous, M. (1998). Integrated care pathways. *BMJ, 316*, 133–137.

DPCM. 24 novembre (2017). Linee guida nazionali per le Aziende sanitarie e le Aziende ospedaliere in tema di soccorso e assistenza socio-sanitaria alle donne vittime di violenza. (18A00520) (G.U. Serie Generale, n. 24 del 30 gennaio 2018).

Gilmore, A. B., Fabbri, A., Baum, F. et al. (2023). Defining and conceptualising the commercial determinants of health. *The Lancet, 401*(10383), April 2023, pp. 1194–1213.

Moro, M. R., & Baubet, T. (2009). Basi della clinica transculturale. In M. R. Moro, Q. De La Noe, Y. Mouchenik, & T. Baube (Eds.), *Manuale di psichiatria transculturale. Dalla clinica alla società*. Milano: Franco Angeli.

Napier, A. D., Ancarno, C., Butler, B., Calabrese, J. et al. (2014). Culture and health (The Lancet Commissions). *The Lancet, 384*(1), 1607–1639.

Reichardt, D. (2020). *Trasculturalismo, Treccani, X Appendice dell'Enciclopedia Italiana di Lettere, Scienze e Arti (former: Parole del XXI Secolo)* (pp. 649–652). Roma.

Vanhaecht, K., De Witte, K., & Sermeus, W. (2007). *The impact of clinical pathways on the organization of care processes*. Leuven: ACCO.

Welsch, W. (2001). Transculturality: The changing form of culture today. *Filozofski vestnik, XXII*(2), 59–86.

World Health Organization. (2013). Responding to intimate partner violence and sexual violence against women: WHO clinical and policy guidelines. Geneva: WHO.

World Health Organization. (2013). London School of Hygiene and Tropical Medicine, South African Medical Research Council: Global and regional estimates of violence against women: Prevalence and health effects of intimate partner violence and non-partner sexual violence. WHO.

World Health Organization. (2013). Violence against women. The Health Sector Responds. Infographics. WHO.

World Health Organization. (2014). Health care for women subjected to intimate partner violence or sexual violence. A clinical handbook WHO/RHR/14.26. Geneva: WHO.

Zimmerman, M. A. (2000). Empowerment theory: Psychological, organizational, and community levels of analysis. In J. Rappaport & E. Seidman (Eds.), *Handbook of community psychology* (pp. 43–63). Kluwer Academic Publishers.

Daniela Belliti

From domination to care. Recognizing and combating the common root of gender violence and environmental degradation

Abstract: In the recent years research has highlighted the link between climate change and gender-based violence. The impact is so significant that the Committee on the Elimination of Violence against Women first introduced the issue in Recommendation No. 35/2017, and then specifically addressed it in Recommendation No. 37/2018. The phenomenon is fuelling the increase in migration flows, in which the female component is preponderant. These data seem to confirm the ecofeminist thesis (since its origin to the latter philosophical development) that there is a link between violence against women and violence against nature; male domination over women, nature, animals rests on the same paradigm of exploitation, abuse and subjugation of the other. If we share this assumption, then a rights approach is not enough to address the problem, but rather a redefinition of relations among living beings is needed, based on a critique of capitalism, a claim for environmental justice and an ethics of care.

Between ecological crisis and gender violence

Since the 1992 Earth Summit in Rio de Janeiro, the international community has increasingly sharpened its focus on the risks of climate change by creating a specific regime of intergovernmental actions at the global level and one of the most prolific interdisciplinary research fields in recent years. In the analysis of the phenomenon and the implementation of mitigation measures, the necessity to adopt a gender perspective emerged very early on. Indeed, women are among the most vulnerable groups to the effects of climate change and environmental degradation, along with children and the elderly. The reasons are well known: behaviours following natural events, the available resources to protect oneself, and the skills that can be activated to adapt or survive are all conditioned by socio-cultural norms that govern a community life. The 2007 Report of the Intergovernmental Panel on Climate Change stated that "one of the expected impacts of climate change is that it could exacerbate existing gender inequalities" (Parry et al., 2007, 458); the gender dimension has to be central in the definition of interventions aimed at increasing adaptive capacity of individuals and systems[1].

This awareness was reinforced at COP[2] 13 in Bali (2007) when the global network of women and feminist activists *Gendercc-Women for Climate Justice* and the *Global Gender & Climate Alliance* were constituted to develop gender-sensitive mitigation and adaptation strategies with women's involvement and participation.

The greater vulnerability of women to climate change is supposed to be the effect of: (a) unequal gender relations; (b) the division of labour that polarises women on care jobs, which are underpaid and linked to territorial permanence, and on agricultural labour, which is more affected by climate; (c) the scarcity of available resources (both material, such as money or water, and immaterial, such as education), (d) limited access to services (social, health services, etc.). The transition from these conditions of discrimination to violence is very short. CEDAW Committee Recommendation No. 35/2017 includes the environment among the factors that can exacerbate violence against women in contexts of displacement, migration, economic globalization, extractive industries and offshoring, militarization, foreign occupation, armed conflict, extremism and terrorism (CEDAW, 2017), and Recommendation No. 37/2018 faces climate change-induced risks and makes proposals inspired by principles of equality and non-discrimination, participation and empowerment, accountability and justice (CEDAW, 2018).

Thanks to the increasing attention of international organizations, the link between climate change, natural disasters and environmental degradation on the one side, and sexual and gender-based violence on the other side, has been analysed in local and regional contexts, in different disciplinary fields ranging from health to law, from sociology to politics, and in comparison with other unprecedented challenges such as the COVID-19 pandemic. All these studies share the gender-sensitive approach of the 2030 Agenda and the Sustainable Development Goals (SDGs); they do not conceal human responsibility for climate change and are aimed at supporting mitigation and adaptation strategies[3]. Studies have found an increase in domestic violence, both due to increased

---

1   Hunter & Emmanuel, 2009; Chindarkar, N. 2012; Moriggi, 2016.
2   COP means Conference Of the Parties of the United Nations Framework Convention on Climate Change, UNFCCC.
3   Castañeda Camey et al., 2020. About international law, Desai & Mandal, 2021. About the juridical regime on climate change, Vithanage, 2023. About the comparison with COVID-19, Agrawal 2023.

intra-familiar tensions resulting from the reduction of natural resources (such as water and food) in contexts where resources are predominantly managed by women and girls (Sawas et al., 2020; Castañeda Camey et al., 2020), and as a result of natural disasters that generate uncertainty, loss of property and basic necessities, post-traumatic stress (Henrici et al., 2010; Parkinson & Zara, 2013; Thurston et al., 2021). Women and girls are more exposed to verbal, physical and sexual violence in refugee and migration contexts, when they are forced to leave their shelter to collect water and food (Zaman, 2020). Practices such as sexual exploitation or early and forced marriage may increase under conditions of scarce resources. Holders of limited available resources may demand sexual services (Gevers et al., 2020); in other cases, a large family may resort to the marriage of daughters to ease the burden of maintenance (HRW, 2015). In contexts of war over the control of natural resources, sexual and gender-based violence is used as a weapon to conquer territory and humiliate the enemy (IRIAD, 2018). Finally, among environmental human rights defenders, there are many women who fight against the unsustainable exploitation of land and natural resources, so that they are exposed to brutal violence, even death[4].

The COP regime, humanitarian agencies and international law have joined forces to develop a complex body of law to mitigate the phenomenon of gender-based violence along with the effects of climate change (Desai & Mandal, 2021). Relying on the additive functioning of humanitarian law, which has gradually added to and complemented its provisions from a gender-oriented perspective, the international community is allocating resources in projects that invest in law, education and sustainable development; in their opinion the governance of climate change also implies combating gender-based violence. But this body of acts and recommendations has a two-fold limitation. First, it is not legally binding; it entrusts national legislation with its implementation without threat of sanctioning regimes. Thus the moderation of the mitigation and adaptation approach is also accompanied by its substantial ineffectiveness.

Secondly, it considers the condition of vulnerability as a factor naturally associated with specific social groups, including women, especially in the contexts of so-called underdeveloped areas. This approach exposes women to the risk of re-victimization, which on the one hand weakens empowerment and change strategies and on the other hand re-proposes binary patterns of analysis (man/woman, human/nature, north/south) with re-perpetuation of unequal and discriminatory power relations.

---

4 https://www.globalwitness.org/en/campaigns/environmental-activists/standing-firm/

Ecofeminism and violence

The gender perspective has become a structural part of climate change mitigation and adaptation policies thanks to the theoretical and practical feminist mobilization, but its normativisation risks to weaken the feminist point of
view's transformative thrust. Since the 1970s critics of the development model
based on extractivism, the fight against the use of civil and military nuclear
power, and concern for future generations, had given rise to women's movements that thematised the nexus between gender and the environment, feminism and ecology.

The term "eco-feminism" was first used by Francoise d'Eaubonne (d'Eaubonne, 1974) in an essay published shortly after the Club of Rome's first denun-
ciation of the unsustainability of the development model (Meadows et al.,
1972). Physical, psychological and economic violence against women and violence against nature, as exploitation and brutalisation of earth, are closely intertwined and have their origin in historical discriminations based on poverty,
race, class, age and gender, constructed by men to keep women excluded from
exercising all kind of power. According to d'Eaubonne, phallocracy is the domination system that men imposed on the world when they discovered to possess
an organ capable of ploughing both the women's body and the earth, expro-
priating women from their primordial agricultural activities and condemning
them only to the reproductive function. Starting from the cultivation of land,
men then moved on to the extraction of resources stored in the earth; the creation of industry alongside agriculture is based on the same phallic production
principle by penetrating, and then deflowering, despoiling, and finally manipu-
lating with technology, both the environmental nature and the feminine nature.
This exploitation culture is also a culture of rape: women, forced to live in fear
of violence, accept submission to men, who defend them from the rape of all
other men but force women to have children for their men. Thus, the phallocen-
tric patriarchal regime based on the double exploitation of women and nature
generates a double burden on earth: overpopulation and resource destruction.
Violence against women cannot be eliminated without eliminating violence
against nature.

> Feminism is the whole of humanity in crisis, the mutation of the species … there is
> no longer any choice; if the world rejects this mutation … it is condemned to death.
> A death that is already around the corner. Not only because of the destruction of the
> ecosystem, but also because of overpopulation, the progress of which passes directly
> from the management of our bodies entrusted to the Male System. (d'Eaubonne, 1974,
> ed.it. 83–84)

Ecofeminism has very different versions, which cannot be recalled here[5]. It is only necessary to emphasise that two main critiques addressed to d'Eaubonne – the essentialism implicit in the idea of a female nature, and the Eurocentrism of the French thinker's world history view – have contributed to new ecofeminist responses, also and especially in developing countries (i.e. Vandana Shiva and her movement Navdanya[6]), more critical of historical processes that led to undesirable outcomes of modernity. Carolyn Merchant identifies the modern science shift from an organicistic to a mechanistic world view as the root of male power over nature; nature was subjugated precisely as mother and nurturer (hence its feminisation and dehumanisation) (Merchant, 1980). According Maria Mies the union of patriarchy and capitalism was a catastrophic alliance for humanity and the planet. In her opinion, capitalism rests on three levels of division (and discrimination): the international division of labour between industrialised and colonised countries; the sexual division of labour between care of home entrusted to women and production outside home entrusted to men; the social division between the public and private spheres, which is also gendered. The Marxist "original accumulation of capital" would still be at work thanks to women's care labour – relegated to invisibility in domestic sphere and therefore unrecognized and unpaid –, to privatization and loss of access to land and common goods, to workers exploitation in the global South and subjugation of nature as such:

> Nature was treated in the same one-sided, exploitative way – as a "free good" – as women's labour or the colonies were treated. To put it the other way round: women and the colonies were treated as "nature", they were "naturalized". (Mies, 1986, p. X)

The common point of all ecofeminist variants is therefore the following: "the ecological crisis is the inevitable effect of a Eurocentric capitalist patriarchal culture built on domination of Nature and domination of Women as Nature" (Salleh, 2017, p. 35).

The various ecofeminist currents have also intervened in the debate on Anthropocene, a concept indicating a new geological epoch marked by human activity. If this idea has already been challenged by a neo-Marxist perspective, according to which humanity as a whole is not responsible for the profound and accelerated changes of our time, but rather capitalist world resting on the intensive and limitless exploitation of natural resources (Capitalocene), feminists change the playing field again: not humanity as such nor the capitalist economy alone is the cause of the crisis, but the male gender, which is responsible

---

5   A syllogy about ecofeminisms is Gaard, 2017 and Marcomin & Cima, 2017.
6   Navdanya (Nine Seeds Movement) fights for seeds and food sovereignty.

for the three forms of separation described above and the resulting domination and exploitation regimes of women, nature and global South. The notion
of Anthropocene is inadequate because it speaks of an undifferentiated gender
subject and confuses the consequences with the causes of ecological crisis; the
causes lie in the patriarchal organization of societies that has imprinted the capitalist economic system (Vuillerod, 2021).

The identification of subjects to be blamed for the ecological crisis (patriarchy,
capitalism, male gender) determine the change strategies that those subjects will
have to take on within a process in which the sphere of law is an instrument and
not the goal of transformation. Alongside the critique of the development model,
feminist movements have also pursued a critique of law, which in their opinion
merely incorporates new subjects into original schemes built around the figure
of white male, without changing the structural basis of domination relationships
(Facchi, 2012). An authentic gendered view, aware of the causes of the crisis, will
not be content to mitigate the effects, but will try to transform reality; it will not
run the risk of "victimising" vulnerable groups, but will make them truly protagonists in the construction of a new ecosystem. In the theoretical and political
projects of ecofeminisms, the participation and empowerment of women are necessary measures, but not sufficient if the change will not affect males, their gender
relations, species and poorer peoples. The "mutation" of which d'Eaubonne spoke
is a true anthropological paradigm shift; indeed, we should coin a neologism that
can indicate together the dimensions of species, gender and cultures.

In the following sections I will outline some research paths: the more properly
eco-feminist one, which aims to change the socio-economic structure of society
with a reconfiguration of the concepts of reproduction and care; the epistemological one of speculative feminism, which redefines the concept of multigen-
der and multi-species nature; the ethical-social one of critical feminism, which
invests in the construction of a vulnerable and interdependent subject.

Reproduction, subsistence and care

The anthropocentric, or rather androcentric, world view, built on dualism man/
nature, mind/body, development/underdevelopment, implied that women, living systems, lands, colonies, were all treated as "nature", i.e. an object to be dominated, exploited and made passive. The cause of the ecological crisis would thus
lie in the male gender's denial of dependence on nature, on bodies, on women's
labour and on the subsistence labour performed in the informal sectors of the
global South: that is, the denial of dependence on the sphere of biological and
social reproduction.

"A change in the existing sexual division of labour would imply first and foremost that the violence that characterizes capitalist-patriarchal man-woman relations worldwide will be abolished not by women, but by men. Men have to refuse to define themselves any longer as Man-the-Hunter. Men have to start movements against violence against women if they want to preserve the essence of their own humanity" (Mies, 1986, 240).

The change lies in an ecological reconversion of economy that values and focuses on the sphere of reproduction and care, as opposed to the sphere of capitalist production that is instead a resources and social relations destruction.

> Only when men begin in earnest to share in care of children, elderly, vulnerables and nature, when they recognise that this subsistence labour to preserve life is more important than labour for money, will they become able to develop an erotic, caring and responsible relationship with their partners, whether male or female. (Mies M. & Shiva V., 1993, 295)

What is needed is a subsistence economy, aimed at creating and recreating life instead of raw materials and surplus value. The concept of reproduction does not only refer to women's domestic labour, but encompasses all the maintaining and preserving natural and social goods labour; its valorization predicts the construction of self-sufficient communities, made up of local care economies and shared management of common goods, as well as ecological and non-violent relations between human and non-human.

Thanks to this enlarged conception of reproduction, ecofeminism has found audience in the theories of de-growth (Herrero, 2012; Latouche, 2018). Otherwise Nancy Fraser, who shares with ecofeminist thought the attribution of responsibility for the ecological crisis to neo-liberal capitalism, which she calls "cannibal" because it is devouring all our dimensions of life and not just the economy, insists on the political battle. According to her, ecological movements focus on "the discriminatory impact of different ecological threats on subaltern populations" without attacking the structural dynamics that underlie not only the inequalities, but the crisis that threatens the whole of humanity. They open up the eco-political perspective to the world, but only with the counter-hegemonic battle to capitalism struggles against despoliation of nature, racial/imperialist dispossession, and exploitation of women can be intertwined (Fraser, 2022, ed. it. 121, 124).

Non-power, only multi gender and multispecies bounds

After denouncing violence against women, nature and the least people of earth, we can and must eliminate it by overthrowing the pedestal of domination that has legitimized it for centuries. Also on this point d'Eaubonne has anticipated paths that others are now taking; it is not a matter of substituting males for power, but of affirming a kind of non-power, i.e. non-hierarchical and horizontal relations, not only between men and women and among human beings, but living beings, animals and plants. Donna J. Haraway shows the most radical thought in this respect. Against the discourse of "phallologocentrism", which places man at the centre of means and self "production", Haraway tries to re-define a concept of "nature" from an epistemological point of view: nature is never separate from human, but as human it is composition, transformation, fiction and fact; it is co-construction of human and non-human, organic and non-organic beings; it is public culture "with many houses and many inhabitants capable of reshaping Earth" (Haraway, 1992, ed.it. 46). Human beings must recognize their dependency in constitution and identity on daily and continuous coexistence with other species, "fellow species" (Haraway, 2008). In the debate over naming of the current era, Haraway goes beyond ecofeminism; she ousts male from the pedestal and the dock, as "at the moment Earth is full of refugees, human and non-human, with no more refuge" (Haraway, 2016, ed.it. 146). She criticizes the term "Anthropocene" because it evokes a belief in restorative technology, as to say that if the human species is responsible for the problem, it will also be able to solve it. Capitalocene, on the other hand, expresses a position of bitter cynicism, according to which the games are already played and the apocalypse is inevitable.

In order to break out of these opposing but equally dangerous pincers, Haraway takes up the feminist (queer, anti-racist, anti-colonialist and anti-capitalist) battle for sexual and reproductive freedom and makes her focus "on the violence that sexual and reproductive orders exert on poor and marginalised people" (Id., 21).

This violence manifests itself both in exploitation of female body for reproductive purposes and in birth control programmes; both serve "the interests of biopolitical states rather than the welfare of women" (Id., 20). But since Haraway shares with d'Eaubonne the judgement on the unsustainability of the demographic bombshell, she thinks the need to re-signify the claim of reproductive and sexual freedom in the decision to have or not to have children. We need a change of perspective in building relationships, outside the patriarchal family towards all the lives within and around us. Far beyond Vandana Shiva's self-sufficient communities, Haraway proposes the "compost communities": symbiogenetic aggregations of living beings that, by developing multi-species environmental justice practices, including the pooling of all newborns, not just humans, help to drastically reduce the number of human beings. Hence the call "Make kin, not babies!", where the term "kin" is emancipated from ties of blood and lineage to include all creatures on Earth. "All creatures share the same 'flesh'"; they are not unrelated individuals, but assemblages of kindred material that we must care for ourselves and for generations to come. Then this epoch will not have to be named according to the subject guilty of the destruction that affects us, but by reknitting the threads that hold together the material of which we are all made, as spiders, bacteria, fungi, jellyfish and so many other species do in order to survive and live on and alongside other beings: Chthulucene (from the California spider Pimoa Chthulu) is the epoch of all time and space that shows us how life happens.

Vulnerability as an ethical resource

The inevitability and at the same time the risk of multi-species coexistence (an infected planet, says Haraway) has emerged powerfully with the COVID-19 pandemic. Judith Butler writes:

> Even without delving into the question of whether the pandemic is a direct or indirect effect of climate change, it seems in any case diriment to place the pandemic condition in the context of climate change, since both make global interdependence a matter of life and death. Whatever sense of the world we wish to privilege in such a discussion, it will in any case be influenced by the issue of current environmental destruction. This means that the pandemic is occurring within a form of "environmental racism", exemplified by the fact that in the poorest parts of the world, water is not drinkable, or by the increasing number of evictions of those without the certainty of an income. The differential relationship that different populations have with air, water, shelter and food – already compromised by climate change and, even before that, by unregulated forms of capitalism – is even more acutely registered under pandemic conditions. Thus, although environmental racism and pandemic constitute distinct situations, they simultaneously connect and, above all, intensify each other. (Butler, 2022, ed.it. 47)

The absence of reference to gender violence in this passage is only apparent. Butler's entire thought is crossed on the one hand by questioning of gender, and on the other by the critique of violence that arises from any normative order, starting with the heterosexual and binary, white and colonial order, which excludes and represses all other differences. The pandemic brought to surface what globalization has tried to conceal: that is, the profound inequalities, and thus the injustices and violence, that criss-cross the planet at all latitudes and have reached such a point that they endanger everyone and everyone together, albeit to different degrees. Butler takes vulnerability as a common condition of the living, in order to make it a lever for new ethical action (Butler, 2004, ed.it. 64). The position of women, who are considered the most vulnerable in ecological crisis, pandemic and emergencies of all kinds, takes on strength; they are no longer victims, but active agents of regeneration and change.

Conclusions

The relationship between ecological crisis and gender-based violence can be investigated through a cause-effect model. All necessary measures will be taken to prevent violence in times of emergency and to implement gender-equitable mitigation and adaptation interventions. This is the meaning of the normative production of the international actors involved in climate change management. But this approach is not only poorly effective, it is also structurally incapable of removing the causes of violence. On the one hand, by assigning women as such the condition of vulnerability, it "naturalises" their role as victims; on the other, by acting on mitigation and not on changing the development model, it does not fully recognize the anthropological nature of the crisis. Ecological and feminist thinking, which thematises the common root of violence against women and nature, overturns the binary and hierarchical approach of climate governance and opens up unprecedented hypotheses of ecological and social change.

References

Agrawal, P., et al. (2023). The interrelationship between food security, climate change, and gender-based violence: A scoping review with system dynamics modeling. *PLOS Global Public Health, 3.*

Castañeda Camey, I., et al. (2020). *Gender-based violence and environment linkages. The violence of inequality.* Gland: IUCN.

Butler, J. (2004). *Precarious life. The powers of mourning and violence.* London, New York: Verso [ed. it. 2004].

Butler, J. (2022). *What world is this? A pandemic phenomenology.* New York: Columbia University Press [ed. it. *Che mondo è questo?* Laterza, Roma-Bari 2023].

CEDAW. (2017). *General recommendation No.35 on gender-based violence against women, updating general recommendation No. 19.*

CEDAW. (2018). *General recommendation No.37 on the gender-related dimensions of disaster risk reduction in the context of climate change.*

Chindarkar, M. (2012). Gender and climate change-induced migration: Proposing a framework for analysis. *Environmental Research Letter.*

Desai, B. H., & Mandal, M. (2021). Role of climate change in exacerbating sexual and gender-based violence against women: A new challenge for International Law. *Environmental Policy and Law, 51,* 137–157.

d'Eaubonne, F. (1974). *Le féminisme ou la mort.* Paris: Femmes en Mouvement [ed. it. *Il femminismo o la morte,* Prospero, Novate Milanese, 2023].

Facchi, A. (2012). A partire dall'eguaglianza. Un percorso nel pensiero femminista sul diritto. *About Gender, 1*, 118–150.

Fraser, N. (2022). *Cannibal Capitalism. How our system is devouring democracy, care and the planet – And what we can do about it.* London, New York: Verso [ed. it. *Capitalismo cannibale*, Laterza, Roma-Bari 2023].

Gaard, G. (2017). *Critical ecofeminism.* Lanham, Boulder, New York, London: Lexington Books.

Gevers, A. et al. (2020). *Why climate change fuels violence against women.* UNDP.

Haraway, D. J. (1992). *The promises of monsters. A regenerative politics for inappropriate/d others.* New York: Routledge [ed. it. *Le promesse dei mostri*, DeriveApprodi, Roma, 2019].

Haraway, D. J. (2008). *When species meet.* University of Minnesota Press.

Haraway, D. J. (2016). *Staying with the trouble. Making Kin in the Chthulucene.* University of Chicago Press, Chicago [ed. it. *Chthulucene. Sopravvivere in un pianeta infetto*, Nero, Roma, 2019].

Henrici, J. M., Helmuth, A. S., & Braun, J. (2010). *Fact sheet: Women, disasters, and Hurricane Katrina.* Washington, DC: IWPR.

HRW. (2015). *Marry before your house is swept away. Child marriage in Bangladesh.*

Herrero, Y. (2012). *Vivir bien con menos. Ajustarse a los limites fisicos con criterios de justicia.* Bilbao: Mau Robles-Arangis Institutua.

Hunter, L. M., & Emmanuel, D. (2009). Climate change and migration: Considering gender dimension. Boulder: *IBS Population Program*, University of Colorado.

IRIAD. (2018). *Conflitti, violenza di genere e sicurezza ambientale.* IRIAD Review. *Studi sulla pace e sui conflitti.*

Latouche, S. (2018). Preface. In F. d'Eaubonne (Rd.), *Ecologie et féminisme. Révolution ou mutation.* Paris : Editions Libre & Solidaire.

Marcomin, F., & Cima, L. (2017). *L'ecofemminismo in Italia. Le radici di una rivoluzione necessaria.* Padova: Il Poligrafo.

Meadows, D. et al. (1972). *The limit to growth.* Washington: Potomac Associates Books.

Merchant, C. (1980). *The death of nature.* New York: Harper & Row.

Mies, M. (1986). *Patriarchy and accumulation in a world scale. Women in the international division of labour.* London: Zed Books.

Mies M., & Shiva V. (1993). *Ecofeminism.* London, New York: Zed Books.

Moriggi, A. (2016). Una prospettiva di genere sui cambiamenti climatici. Vulnerabilità e adattamento, discorso internazionale e gender mainstreaming. *DEP. Rivista telematica di studi sulla memoria femminile, 30*, 38–57.

Parry, M. et al. (ed.). (2007). *Climate Change 2007: Impacts, Adaptation and Vulnerability. Contribution of Working Group II to the Fourth Assessment Report of the Intergovernmental Panel on Climate Change.* IPCC, Cambridge University Press.

Parkinson, D., & Zara, C. (2013). The hidden disaster: domestic violence in the aftermath of natural disaster. *The Australian Journal of Emergency Management.*

Salleh, A. (2017). *Ecofeminism as politics: Nature, Marx and the Postmodern.* London: Zed Books.

Sawas, A. et al. (2020). Reflections on gender, climate, and security linkages in urban Pakistan. In UN Women and UNEP, *Gender, Climate & Security: Sustaining inclusive peace on the frontlines of climate change, 36.*

Shiva, V. (1991). *Ecology and the politics of survival: Conflicts over natural resources in India.* Vandana Shiva et al., United Nations University Press.

Thurston, A. M. et al. (2021). Natural hazards, disasters and violence against women and girls: A global mixed-methods systematic review. *BMJ Global Health.*

Vithanage, A. C. (2023). Addressing correlations between gender-based violence and climate change: An expanded role for International Climate Change Law and Education for Sustainable Development. *Pace Environmental Law Review, 38,* 327–382.

Vuillerod, J. (2021). L'Anthropocène est un Androcène: trois perspectives écoféministes. *Nouvelles Questions Féministes, 40,* 18–34.

Zaman, S. (2020). Climate change induced gender-based violence against women during water collection: A case study in Shatkhira Upazilla Bangladesh. *Cap-Net Bangladesh.*

Maria Lucia Piga and Patrizia Desole[1]

The great destruction: Violence against women, against the planet, against all life

Abstract: The environmental crisis and violence against women are among the crucial issues that afflict contemporary society, both because of the violence they imply and because of the widening gap in inequalities. Although the two dimensions may seem distant and distinct (macro and micro respectively), environmental damage and violence against women are actually two sides of a single coin, a sword of Damocles hanging over the whole of humanity and the survival of the planet with its biodiversity. The great destruction sees women not only more exposed to violence (such as in the practice of *sex-for-fish* or in the coal trade in Congo) but also as activists on the front line to defend their territories (e.g. Nemonte Nenquimo, Licypriya Kangujam, Greta Thumberg). Consider also about protest of Afghan and Iranian women (*Woman Life Freedom*), as well as the journalist often killed when they get in the way of corruption, from Ilaria Alpi to Anna Politkovskaya. Faced with these problems, which are intertwined in a spiral of increasing gravity, what policies are possible, locally and globally? Beyond the apocalyptic scenarios, what solutions for sustainable development can pave the way for a change, in the perspective of solidarity with future generations? The aim of this work is to investigate the links between environmental crisis and the destructive violence; at the same time, it highlights multidisciplinary tools – including ecofeminist thought, indigenous feminism movements and the critique of biopower – that question the patriarchal order and advanced capitalism, from whose recurrent crises these forms of violence seem to derive.

Introduction

The environmental crisis and violence against women are among the crucial issues afflicting contemporary society, both due to the violence and the widening gap of inequalities created by the capitalistic system. Although these two dimensions may seem distant and distinct, environmental damage and violence against women are actually two sides of the same coin, a sword of Damocles hanging over humanity and the survival of the planet with its biodiversity. The

---

1 This article is the result of a joint work, however it is due to Piga the writing of Introduction and Conclusions, to Desole all the rest.

great destruction sees women not only more exposed to violence but also as the primary activists in their own territories. Faced with such problems, which intertwine in a spiral of increasing severity, what tools of resistance, forms of struggle, and policies are possible? Beyond apocalyptic scenarios, what sustainable development solutions can pave the way for a change of course, in the perspective of solidarity with future generations? The purpose of this work is to shed light on the connections between the environmental crisis and violence against women, while also highlighting the need for innovative and multidisciplinary theoretical contributions – including ecofeminist thought – with a critical view towards the patriarchal order and capitalism, from which these forms of violence seem to stem. The first paragraph explores both phenomena, that of violence against women and environmental changes, highlighting the connections between them. The second paragraph analyses ecofeminist thought and its role in denouncing the common matrix of gender inequality and environmental destruction. The third focuses on the fundamental role played by ecofeminists and activists worldwide in counteracting both phenomena. Finally, in the conclusions, some core points of female resistance to the great destruction are highlighted, as well as possible points of arrival of critical ecofeminist thought to counteract it, towards a vision centred on women's thinking, that builds a culture of caring for the planet.

Environmental crisis and violence against women: For a based-gender reading

Gender-based violence against women is a global, complex, pervasive, social and structural phenomenon. It is deeply ingrained and multidimensional, affecting millions of girls and women across age groups, social classes, ethnicities, and sexual orientations. Aproximately 379 million women worldwide have experienced physical and/or sexual violence. Additionally, in conflict areas, the percentages of such situations are higher than the global average. The World Health Organization (WHO) considers violence against women a public health issue and identifies it as one of the main risk factors for the health and mortality of women and girls. Furthermore, the WHO reports that violence against women is a global phenomenon of immense proportions and indicates that 38 % of femicides worldwide are committed by intimate partners. From these empirical findings, gender-based violence manifests itself in many different forms, all deeply rooted in the social structure.

Gender-based violence in its structural dynamics

Feminist studies have emphasized the gendered and structural connotation of violence against women, considering it a violation of human rights. The Istanbul Convention (hereinafter IC), in its preamble, recognizes its gender-based structural nature as one of the crucial mechanisms through which women are coerced into a subordinate position, relative to men. It highlights that women and girls are more exposed to gender-based violence, such as domestic violence, forced marriages, genital mutilation, and honour-based violence. According to the IC, all these forms of violence are severe violations of human rights and hinder the achievement of gender equality. Addressing this issue effectively requires the adoption of policies and the establishment of legal, cultural, and social frameworks, as well as support services capable of countering the phenomenon in a radical and structural manner. This involves not only prevention, protection, punishment, and integrated policies (the 4 P's, key elements of the IC) but also delving into its root causes. Responses to a structural problem cannot be solely emergency-based; it is necessary to act on the social representations of gender roles and relationships, to dismantle the acceptability of violent behaviour, and prevent processes of victimization. With which tools can we capture the connections and implications between gender-based violence, environmental and climate changes, resource exploitation, biodiversity destruction, and conflicts?

An intersectional approach will be useful in recognizing the interweaving and affinities of various oppressions, including sexism, classism, racism, etc. Furthermore, it is imperative and urgent to consider colonialism and biopiracy (Shiva, 1999). Only recently the reading of violence against women was considered by international organizations in its gender specificity. The definition of gender-based violence was adopted by the UN General Assembly only when the "Declaration on the Elimination of Violence against Women" was passed with Resolution 48/104, on Dec 20th, 1993, marking it as one of the most significant documents on the subject[2], alongside the IC and the 2030 Agenda. The feminist movement played a significant role in implementing these important tools, emphasizing the empowerment of women and the importance of adopting the gender mainstreaming.

---

2 https://www.un.org/documents/ga/res/48/a48r104.htm

The two sides of the same coin

The issue of sustainable development encouraged scholars to consider the connections between seemingly distinct phenomena and to generate recommendations for preventing violence (Owren, 2021), thus creating a new paradigm for addressing the new challenges of globalized society and the emergence of crucial issues for our survival: conflicts, environmental and climate changes, poverty, and gender-based violence. "Today, complex human organizations are required to radically shift development models and guide them with innovative strategies: to replace purely economic objectives with social ones, and to have a perspective that considers not only the present but also the future" (Nocenzi, 2022: 299).

A recent study conducted by the IUCN (International Union for Conservation of Nature) non-governmental organization, highlighted the strong impact of environmental and climate changes in exacerbating violence against women and the gender gap[3]. The study, based on the analysis of over 80 case studies and more than 1000 sources, appears to be the most comprehensive research to date that correlates these aspects. In this regard, Grethel Aguilar (IUCN Acting Director General) stated:

> This study shows us that the harm humanity is inflicting on nature can also fuel violence against women worldwide, a link that has largely been overlooked... This study adds urgency to stopping environmental degradation, encompassing all actions aimed at stopping gender-based violence in all its forms, and demonstrates that these two issues must often be addressed together[4].

The research revealed, in addition to the complex nature of violence and its interconnections with other dramatic phenomena such as environmental and climate disasters, how it manifests in specific contexts where associated problems of scarcity and strategic resource control, environmental damage, and environmental defence actions are present. The study highlighted that in all these situations, there is a significant gender gap, and violence against women is widespread, also due to traditional norms regulating gender inequality in access to and control of resources, thus normalizing privileges and causing exclusion and perpetuating the marginalization of women. Another dramatic aspect, widespread in some parts of the world, is the presence of criminal organizations dedicated to

---

3   https://portals.iucn.org/library/files/documents/2020-002-En.pdf. See also: https://www.wired.it/attualita/ambiente/2020/01/30/ambiente-clima-violenza-donne-studio/
4   https://www.iucn.org/news/gender/202001/environmental-degradation-driving-gender-based-violence-iucn-study

sexual exploitation precisely in contexts where violence against nature is more pronounced: when resources are scarce (primarily water, due to drought), conflicts are harsh for control over them. There is also the exploitation of valuable resources, with practices such as poaching, illegal trade of minerals, and rare living species. In these cases, gender-based violence and ethnic conflicts serve the social disorder that allows criminal organizations to exert control over individuals, communities, and territory.

Various studies highlighted the greater likelihood of girls and women experiencing violence in contexts where water is scarce. In many countries such as sub-Saharan Africa, Pakistan, Tanzania, Ethiopia, Uganda, and Mexico, it is the responsibility of girls and women to provide water for the family's daily needs, exposing them to the risk of physical violence, harassment, and sexual violence during their journeys. There is also evidence that many girls and young women do not attend school due to this particular form of exploitation of female and child labour. Another example of violence against women linked to resource scarcity is the so-called practice of "fish-for-sex" prevalent in some areas of Africa: fishermen sell fish to women on the condition of engaging sexual abuses in return. In Southeast Asia, for instance, in the fishing sector, sexual exploitation of women and girls is present, often with the complicity of local authorities. In the Republic of Congo, as well as in Brazil, Paraguay, Colombia, Peru, and Indonesia, illegal mineral extraction and deforestation are associated with sexual violence and sexual trafficking. In Southeast Asia, for example, women are forced into forced prostitution by those engaged in these illegal activities. There is empirical evidence demonstrating that in those countries – unprepared to face disasters due to climate change (whose political, economic, and social organization is found to be inadequate for the problem) – violence against women increases exponentially, also due to the lack of public services that can prevent the problem.

Contexts generating violence

Girls and women are found to be the most affected by the consequences of ecological disasters and climate change. Experts have observed that violence against women is prevalent among environmental refugees and migrants. Additionally, it has been noted that activists, journalists, and environmentalists are at risk of experiencing violence or being killed in regions afflicted by environmental crimes and disasters.

In 2019, a team of experts from Stanford University argued that "The intensification of climate change will elevate the future risk of violent armed conflicts

within countries"[5]. Similarly, Miles-Novelo and Anderson (2019) contend that
violence will escalate, because the "eco-migration" creates intergroup conflicts
over resources, which can lead to political violence, civil wars, or wars between
nations (Mazzantini, 2019). In analysing the connection between gender and
environmental/climate changes, factors such as division of labour, unequal access
to resources resulting in the "feminization of poverty", gender norms, and limited access to decision-making processes emerge, highlighting women's greater
vulnerability. This makes it evident that the impact of environmental and climate
changes is more burdensome for women. A study from the IUCN, after examining 141 natural disasters in various countries around the world, emphasized
the importance of adopting a gender perspective. It revealed that where wom-
en's social and economic rights are denied, environmental and climate disasters
have a disproportionately negative impact on them (Castañeda et al., 2020). An
example is the cyclone that struck Bangladesh in 1991: the disaster claimed the
lives of 140,000 people, with 90 % of them being women. It happened indeed
that the alarm was primarily raised in markets, places restricted to women due
to persisting inequitable gender norms. Similarly, a gendered approach was not
considered in the post-disaster response. The reception for displaced persons did
not consider women and their specific needs: privacy, pregnancy, breastfeeding,
and women who, due to the overcrowded and unprotected environment, were at
risk of experiencing violence and sexual abuse (Moriggi, 2016).

These aspects have devastating repercussions not only for women but also
for the most vulnerable individuals and poorer countries, which bear less
responsibility for climate change and environmental disasters. This leads to a
climate apartheid, where the wealthy pay to escape from overheating, hunger,
and conflicts while the rest of the world remains to suffer (Campana, 2023).
Consequently, it underscores our awareness of how impactful these phenomena
are, which, despite their specificities, are interconnected.

Ecofeminism: A powerful thought to make the world better

It is thanks to ecofeminist thought that the common root of gender oppression
and extreme/brutal exploitation of natural resources has been revealed. This paradigm has deepened the connections within this binomial and unmasked the
complex power structures that determine a condition of subordination, greater

---

5   see https://retepacedisarmo.org/educazione-pace/2023/conflitti-e-migranti-laltra-fac
    cia-della-crisi-climatica/

vulnerability, and a higher risk of experiencing violence in contexts as described above (Kaijser & Kronsell, 2014; Mac Gregor, 2009). Especially in recent decades, various ecofeminist-inspired women's movements have emerged worldwide with the goal of raising awareness about the link between gender and the environment, between the destruction of nature and violence against women. According to this frame, these oppressions share common roots within both patriarchy and capitalism. Among the pioneers of this thought, Françoise d'Eaubonne must be considered. In 1974, she coined the term "ecofeminism" and, even in those years, warned about the risks of a destructive trend caused by human activity on the planet. She also attributed the responsibility for the environmental crisis to the patriarchal and capitalist system. According to her opinion, it is imperative to counterpose ecofeminist thought to this system: "considering feminism on a much broader plane than conceived thus far, exploring how the modern crisis resulting from the struggle between the sexes connects to a general change, or a new humanism, the only remaining salvation" (D'Eaubonne, 2022). So, ecofeminism, highly critical of the current socio-economic development model, pushes the international community to consider this link and identify sustainable and inclusive alternatives.

Over the years, many feminist scholars have analysed the relationship between women and the environment from different perspectives. Among them, Australian sociologist Ariel Salleh (2017) stands out as one of the leading interpreters of ecofeminism, known for her analysis of the relationship between patriarchy, capitalism, and globalization. In Salleh's vision, capitalism is nothing more than the modern version of patriarchy, embracing a highly critical position towards eurocentrism and anthropocentrism: her political model is not essentialist, but it is based on an open critique of patriarchy and capitalism. In the same point of view, Vandana Shiva emphasizes how women and the environment are common victims of the neocolonialism development model, while Mary Fellow and Marilyn Waring attribute the correlation between gender discrimination and environmental destruction to the social reproductive role played by women. Additionally, Carolyn Merchant, in her famous essay *The Death of Nature* criticizes rationalism, and also a certain representation of nature, that justifies and allows for the systematic depletion of resources, as well as the exploitation of animals and dominion over women. This has led to the death of nature, upon which a new source of well-being is imposed, the technological one. Carol Adams, in her book *The Sexual Politics of Meat*, develops the concept of the "consumable body" to explain the connection between animal slaughter and rape. This leads to both the dehumanization of the victim and an ontological transformation: from a living being to a mere object of consumption.

Laura Cima is one of the leading proponents of ecofeminism in Italy, arguing for the primacy of a circular, feminine thought over linear male thought, which dominates everything: women, nature, and the most vulnerable. She advocates for overturning a model of a pyramidal societal structure with the white male at the top, and asserting a thought that breaks closed spheres, that enriches itself with differences, seeking connections among them.

The ecofeminist movement also developed in the United States. In 1980, the conference "Women and Life on Earth" was organized at the University of Massachusetts, on the initiative of Ynestra King. In 1987, she wrote an article titled *What is Ecofeminism?* in which she urges Americans, in particular, to reflect on the entrenched belief system that simultaneously allows the senseless exploitation of the planet's resources and the oppression of women.

This brief overview does not exhaust all the ecofeminist elaborations that have attempted to challenge the system of domination over nature and women worldwide. It is important to note that many of these ecofeminist activists and scholars come from the Global South. In addition to the previously mentioned Shiva, figures like Bina Agarwal and Arundhati Roy from India, and others from Africa such as Wangari Maathai and Shanysa Khasiani, should be remembered. A comprehensive discussion would be warranted on the thought-provoking, innovative, and radical reflections of Donna Haraway, one of the most significant contemporary feminist and ecological theorists (also known as the founder of cyberfeminism). In her theory of multi-species alliance, she constructs a truly original thought that transcends anthropocentrism, aiming to build a shared relationship involving all species. She adopts a multidisciplinary approach, also starting with a deconstruction of language through the use of neologisms, i.e. *Cthulucene*[6], that make it challenging to grasp her thought. According to Haraway, it is necessary to think, embracing Hannah Arendt's invitation, "from experiences, but involving all species. A thought shared with them". Her reference to Arendt shows the symbolic leap that she suggests and that we are experiencing in the age of ecofeminist revolution. Today, the possibility of making a clear turn that can save the planet lies in creating networks with all species, human and non-human (Zamboni, 2020).

Ecofeminism has played a significant role worldwide in raising awareness of the seriousness of the situation and in stressing the urgency to step in a different

---

6   This expression derives from the name of the California spider *Pimoa Cthulu*, by which Haraway refers to our era, characterized by dense and invisible subterranean connections between human, beyond human, inhuman.

drummer, without reducing the problem to essentialist and spiritualist theory (Moriggi, 2016). Therefore, there is a need for empirical studies that not only analyse the specificity of the context but also relate these aspects that we have explored above, in different countries and contexts, for example, in the Western world. From this perspective, sociological research would be of great help, provided that one considers ecofeminist thought and a multidisciplinary approach, i.e. Clarke's situational analysis could be useful (Cersosimo, 2022). In addition to this, the intersectional approach could provide – by a deeper understanding of the described dynamics and connections – some radical horizons of knowledge. In conclusion, it can be generally stated that ecofeminism, being both a theoretical and activist movement, has concretely influenced the creation of real points of resistance, especially in contexts where the effects of environmental changes have had a greater negative impact on women.

Women's resistance small groups worldwide to counteract massive destruction

Today, women continue to fight for their rights and for environmental protection, at the cost of their lives, in defending their lands and their rights. Women's organizations worldwide are a sign of hope for the future. As mentioned earlier, many of them have been killed precisely for their resistance to both patriarchal and capitalist or military power dynamics. Like the journalist Ilaria Alpi, killed in 1994 for her investigations into toxic waste and arms trafficking in Somalia, or the activist Berta Flores, killed in 2016 in Honduras after fighting alongside other women against the privatization of rivers by multinational corporations. Recently, many others have been killed, such as Estela Casanto Mauricio in Peru, who fought to defend her land from resource plunderers. Think of Afghan and Iranian women, killed and imprisoned. What gives further hope is that many of these women activists are very young, some even children, like the Nobel Peace Prize Malala Yousafzai or the eco activist Greta Thunberg.

The list is very long; women and girls around the world do not stop, despite the risks of experiencing violence, abuse, attacks, and even the risk of being killed. They represent a vanguard in the protection of the environment, biodiversity, pollution, climate change, food security, activists in counteracting violence against women, demanding a radical change and concrete perspectives. In June of this year, in Rome, women from all over the world, in the presence of authoritative scholars and activists (including Shiva), drafted the *Ecofeminist Manifesto, making Peace with the Earth*. The *Green Belt,* the *Love Canal,* and the *Chipko Movements* are formed by women activists. With their form of nonviolent and risky struggle, the *Chipko* activists embrace the trees that loggers cut down in the forests of the Himalayas, carrying out not only a political struggle but also a re-resistance to environmental destruction through the re-appropriation of the work of care of planet, thus also caring for the souls of individuals that the consumptive and masculinist development model has brought to self-destruction. The United Nations (UN), while recognizing women's greater vulnerability to climate change and disasters, but at the same time their key role in fundamental environmental defence and in promoting eco-sustainability. However, they are still excluded from decision-making processes. Finally, it is crucial to remove the barriers that prevent them from fully participating in the sustainable management of ecosystems for the survival of the planet.

Conclusions

The challenges of the environmental crisis, gender inequality, and the consequent connection between these aspects lead to an increase in violence against women. This link can no longer be overlooked but requires approaches and tools that radically rethink the foundations of society and the economy. Moreover, according to Shiva (2023), a profound transformation of language is necessary: to interconnect and rediscover the value of certain words that can change the world in the name of creative power and regeneration, in order to dismantle the logic of the power of violent domination (think of wars as the end of politics) and orient our imagination towards radically new paths for a care-based economy and a democracy of the earth. New practices and new intercultural relationships are needed, along with the meeting of visions and thoughts whose peculiar and critical approaches allow us to understand the complexity and new connections necessary to address innovative changes and a new ecofeminist development idea. As several scholars have emphasized, academic analysis and commitment can encompass a broader level that goes beyond the abstract sphere, but delves into intersectional sociological analysis open to multidisciplinary contaminations and the contribution of critical feminist posthumanism, with an approach that knows how to practice gender mainstreaming. For example, an interesting and useful meeting point can be identified in the "meridian thought" of sociologist Cassano and the ecofeminist thought of Shiva. Both have focussed in-depth on economic-cultural predation and colonization by the Global North towards the Global South and on other "fundamental issues such as the diversity of worldviews, the relationship between progress and technological development, the ecological crisis, and the production of new cultural values" (Biancofiore, 2017: 162). Both of these thoughts highlight the urgency of "establishing criteria

of judgment other than those that currently dominate, thinking of another rul-
ing class, another grammar of poverty and wealth, thinking of the dignity of
another form of life" (Cassano, 1996: 6–7). They emphasize the importance of
opening up to dialogue and intercultural practices. It is no coincidence that
Shiva wrote the book *Ecofeminism* with Maria Mies, a German researcher, creating bridges between cultures and common rights, empowerment of women and
the safeguarding of life on the planet. Consequently, Shiva asserts that "only by
choosing the path of care, in reverence of the Earth, will we bequeath a better
world to future generations". *From Greed to Care*: these concepts should be bor-
rowed, enriched, and translated into a "theoretical political agenda" capable of
addressing these complex issues, particularly by translating them into policies
that have an impact at the meso level, beyond macro-level strategies and policies.
Finally, there should be no fear of embracing radical and entirely novel positions,
such as the Donna Haraway's vision: in the era of transhumanism and faced with
the risk of dystopian scenarios, the time has come to seize this opportunity for a
posthuman ethics that preserves the life and harmony of all living beings.

References

Biancofiore, A. (2017). Quando il Sud e il Nord s'incontrano: nuove pratiche
interculturali. *Narrativa*, n. 39. Available at https://etudesromanes.parisn
anterre.fr/publications/nuove-frontiere-del-sud (last consultation November
15th, 2023).

Campana, A. (2023). Conflitti e migranti. L'altra faccia della crisi climatica.
#EducazionePace. Available at https://retepacedisarmo.org/educazione-pace/
2023/conflitti-e-migranti-laltra-faccia-della-crisi-climatica/ (last consultation November 15th, 2023).

Castañeda Carney, I., Sabater, L., Owren, C., & Boyer, A. E. (2020). *Gender-based
violence and environment linkages*. IUCN Publication, Gland, Switzerland.
Available at https://portals.iucn.org/library/node/48969 (last consultation
November 11th, 2023).

Cassano, F. (1996). *Il pensiero meridiano*. Bari: Laterza.

Cersosimo, G. (Ed.). (2022). *Adele Clarke. From Grounded Theory to situational
analysis. Implicitly feminist methods*. Lecce: Edizioni Kurumuny.

D'Eaubonne, F. (2022). *Il femminismo o la morte. Il manifesto dell'ecofemminismo*.
Milano: Prospero Editore.

Kaijser, A., & Kronsell, A. (2014). Climate change through the lens of intersectionality. *Environmental Politics, 23*(3), 417–433.

MacGregor, S. (2009). A stranger silence still: The need for feminist social research on climate change. *The Sociological Review*, n. 57, 124–140.

Miles-Novelo, A., & Anderson, C. A. (2019). Climate change and psychology: Effects of rapid global warming on violence and aggression. *Current Climate Change Reports*, 5, 36–46. https://doi.org/10.1007/s40641-019-00121-2. Available at Gli eco-migranti del cambiamento climatico. Aumenta il potenziale di conflitti e violenza – Greenreport: economia ecologica e sviluppo sostenibile (last consultation November 15th, 2023).

Mazzantini, U. (2019). Gli eco-migranti del cambiamento climatico. Aumenta il potenziale di conflitti e violenza. *Greenreport.it*. Available at https://greenrep ort.it/news/clima/gli-eco-migranti-del-cambiamento-climatico-aumenta-il-potenziale-di-conflitti-e-violenza/ (last consultation November 15th, 2023).

Moriggi, A. (2016). Una prospettiva di genere sui cambiamenti climatici. Vulnerabilità e adattamento, discorso internazionale e gender mainstreaming. *DEP Deportate, Esuli, Profughe. Rivista telematica di studi sulla memoria femminile*, n. 30 (38–57). Available at https://www.unive.it/pag/fileadmin/user _upload/dipartimenti/DSLCC/documenti/DEP/numeri/n30/03_Ric_Mori ggi.pdf (last consultation November 15th, 2023).

Nocenzi, M. (2022). Nuove prospettive di ricerca. Sostenibilità e società transculturale. In F. Corbisiero e M. Nocenzi (a cura di). *Manuale di educazione al genere e alla sessualità* (pp. 298–305). Novara: UTET.

Owren, C. (2021). Understanding and addressing gender-based violence as part of the climate emergency. *EGM/ENV/EP*. 8, September 2021. Available at https://anrows.intersearch.com.au/anrowsjspui/bitstream/1/20809/1/Cate_ 20OWREN_CSW66_20Expert_20Paper.pdf (last consultation November 15th, 2023).

Salleh, A. (2017). *Ecofeminism as Politics: Nature, Marx and the Postmodern*. London: Zed Books.

Shiva, V. (1999). *Biopirateria. Il Saccheggio della Natura e dei Saperi Indigeni*. Napoli: CUEN.

Shiva, V. (2023). *Parole che cambiano il mondo*. Bologna: EMI.

Zamboni, C. (2020). Chthulucene. Sopravvivere su un pianeta infetto di Donna Haraway. *Per amore del mondo*, n. 17. Available at https://www.diotimafilos ofe.it/wp-content/uploads/2021/03/Donna-Haraway.pdf (last consultation November 15th, 2023).

Angela Di Stasi and Anna Iermano

"Climate Violence", gendered migration, and women's health: What relationship and what protection?

Abstract: This chapter focuses on the "Climate violence", that is part of the complex array of dimensions of violence against women and girls, with a particular manifestation that inevitably affects their psychophysical health. In particular, climate change compel women and girls to leave their countries of origin, disrupting their lives. In this context, the issue of women's access to health services, reproductive health, and psychosocial support services is undoubtedly crucial. However, in order to move away from considering women merely as "victims" of climate change, efforts are being made at the international level to increase their participation in the formulation and implementation of policies and action plans to respond to climate change and disasters, to reduce the risks, and to influence the decisions in this regard.

Introductory remarks: Climate violence as a gendered phenomenon and (possible) cause of female migration and slow violence

"Climate violence" is part of the complex array of dimensions of violence against women and girls, with a particular manifestation that inevitably affects their psychophysical health[1].

---

1   As well known, health protection was first recognized internationally in the preamble to the WHO Constitution of 22 July 1946 then recalled by the Universal Declaration of Human Rights (10 December 1948, Resolution No. 217-A of 09/12/1948, Art. 25). For further information, see S. Tonolo, D. Monego (2023). Il diritto alla salute delle donne migranti: garanzie costituzionali e internazionali a confronto. In A. Di stasi, R. Cadin, A. Iermano, V. Zambrano (eds.), *Donne migranti e violenza di genere nel contesto giuridico internazionale ed europeo/Migrant women and gender-based violence in the international and european legal framework*. Napoli: Editoriale Scientifica, p. 371 ss.

Hannah Arendt argued that violence in general is the most obvious manifestation of power, a social construct rather than a natural attribute of human beings[2]. Indeed, it permeates society at the international level, manifesting in relations between States, and at the private level, in everyday interpersonal relations.

From this perspective, violence is not a "natural" phenomenon, but rather a tool for maintaining power relations that have been entrenched and reproduced in society over time. It is a social construct that perpetuates patterns of discrimination, including intersectional discrimination against women.

In particular, the term "climate violence" used in this work is based on the fact that, on the one hand, climate change is a consequence of a set of situations caused by humanity – or at least by part of it[3] – including violence perpetrated by humans against other species. On the other hand, it refers to forms of violence, including gender-based violence against women, which may be exacerbated precisely because of climate change.

In essence, these factors contribute to reinforcing existing forms of discrimination within society and to the materialization of violent phenomena. In this respect, understanding the causes of the disproportionate impact of climate change on women enables formulating hypotheses for responding to migration facilitated by these phenomena.

In fact, climate is never the sole cause of migration, but is often "socially mediated"[4] and includes other forms of slow violence, referring to a seemingly invisible form of violence[5], although its effects are felt both by people, in an intra- and intergenerational perspective, and by nature. It can indeed lead to environmental disasters, but its peculiarity lies in its gradual manifestation, which is why it is often overlooked, even from a legal point of view, in the current logic. Indeed, it

---

2   H. Arendt (2008) [1970]. *Sulla violenza*. Parma, p. 90.

3   G. Gaard (1993). Living Interconnections with Animals and Nature. In G. Gaard (ed.), *Ecofeminism. Women, Animals, Nature*. Philadelphia, p. 1.

4   P. Lama, M. Hamza, M. Wester (2021). Gendered Dimensions of Migration in Relation to Climate Change. *Climate and Development*, 2021, n. 13, 4, pp. 326–336, in particular, p. 329.

5   Violence is often understood as an event or action that occurs at a particular time in history, such as a natural disaster. International disaster law focuses on the legal issues arising from the prevention, response and recovery of various natural disasters, as well as man-made disasters such as major industrial accidents. See, *inter alia*, F. Zorzi Giustiniani (2021). *International Law in Disaster Scenarios – Applicable Rules and Principles*. Cham; L. Bakošová, M. Scott (2020). *Climate Change, Disasters, and the Refugee Convention*. Cambridge.

can be legally interpreted from a number of perspectives: in terms of obligations under international conventions[6], in terms of applicable principles, including those of international environmental law, and in terms of violations of fundamental human rights[7]. Examples include climate change, but also permafrost thawing, ocean acidification, deforestation, rising sea levels, the use of pesticides and substances such as mercury[8].

Notes on the gendered nature of migration as a result of climate change

Climate change, as an apparently neutral phenomenon[9], can exacerbate situations of discrimination, including gender discrimination, that already exist in societies[10]. It is therefore a social phenomenon that can constitute a form of

---

6   See, for example, the Paris Agreement on Climate Change, the Montego Bay Convention on Marine Pollution and the 2001 Stockholm Convention on Persistent Organic Pollutants.

7   On the relationship between war, peace, and ecology, see E. Cusato (2021). *The Ecology of War and Peace*. Cambridge.

8   The reference is to Minamata disease, which developed in the Japanese city of the same name. As the *Special Rapporteur on the implications for human rights of the environmentally sound management and disposal of hazardous substances and wastes* noted in his report of 2022: "*Women and girls aged 14–45 years are particularly vulnerable to the neurotoxic impact of mercury. (...) In utero exposure to mercury at very low levels can result in significant IQ deficits and developmental disorders. If mothers have highly elevated mercury levels, their children can be born with deformities, severe cognitive impairment, and symptoms reported in Minamata disease such as paraesthesia, ataxia, dysarthria, tremors, and constriction of visual fields, or "tunnel vision*". Cfr. *Mercury, small-scale gold mining and human rights*, A/HRC/51/35, 8 July 2022. About the writer Michiko Ishimure, who documented the effect of mercury in Minimata, see M. Mizutamari (2020). Michiko Ishimure e i "popoli nomadi". *Deportate, Esuli e Profughe*, 2020, n. 41–42, pp. 125–134.

9   International regulation of climate-induced migration is a relatively recent development. Until 2010, the international community was virtually 'silent' on the issue. In fact, it was in that year that the member states of the United Nations Framework Convention on Climate Change (UNFCCC) acknowledged the existence of the problem for the first time.

10 On this point, see S. De Vido (2023). In dubio pro futuris generationibus: una risposta giuridica eco-centrica alla slow violence. In M. Frulli (ed.), *L'interesse delle future generazioni nel diritto internazionale e dell'Unione europea*, Atti del Convegno SIDI. Napoli: Editoriale Scientifica; E. Fornalé (2024). Parità di genere e cambiamenti

gender-based violence against women. Like other phenomena of environmental degradation caused by parts of humanity, it contributes to shaping migratory flows and is one of the reasons why groups of people are forced to leave their country of origin.

Over the past decade, the link between climate change and migration has received increasing attention from legal scholars[11]. Although the exact figures on the extent of the phenomenon remain controversial[12], there seems to be broad consensus that climate change has a significant impact on, and is a relevant factor in, human mobility[13].

Indeed, as early as 2016, the New York Declaration for Refugees and Migrants, as well as the documents of numerous international organizations, such as IOM,[14] recognized that migration also occurs in response to climate change, natural disasters, or other environmental factors[15].

However, the response so far has not been as decisive from a gender perspective, aimed at understanding the dramatic nature and impact not only of major

---

climatici in tempi di "polycrisis". In A. Di Stasi (ed.), *Dalla non discriminazione alle pari opportunità. Un itinerario di confronto, ricerca e sperimentazione di buone prassi a UNISA… e oltre. Atti del Convegno internazionale di studi tenuto in occasione della Giornata internazionale della donna 2023*. Milano: Ledizioni, p. 117 ss., in particular, p. 118 pointing out "the violence of "nature" is discriminatory".

11 For further bibliographical references, see, *inter alia* J. McAdam (ed.) (2010). *Climate Change and Displacement: Multidisciplinary Perspectives*. Oxford; S. Behrman, A. Kent (eds.) (2018). *Climate Refugees: Beyond the Legal Impasse?* Abingdon/New York; G. Sciaccaluga (2020). *International Law and the Protection of Climate Refugees*. Cham.

12 On the difficulty of reconstructing accurate estimates of the scale of the phenomenon of climate-induced migration, see the work of A. Randall. *Climate Refugees: How Many are there? How Many will there be?*, available at the link http://climatemigration.org. uk/climate-refugees-how-many/

13 See, for example, D. Ionesco et al. (2018). *The Atlas of Environmental Migration*. Abingdon/New York.

14 See, for example, IOM (2014). A Gender Approach to Environmental Migration, Brief n. 13. *IOM Outlook on Migration, Environment and Climate Change*, Ginevra, 2014, https:// publications. iom. int/ system/files/pdf/mecc_outlook.pdf; UNHCR (2022). *Gender, Displacement and Climate Change*. Ginevra, https://reporting.unhcr.org/ document/3568; UN Women (2022). *Explainer: How Gender Inequality and Climate Change are Interconnected*, https://www.unwomen. org/en/news-stories/explainer/ 2022/02/explainer-how-gender-inequality-and-climate-change-are-interconnected.

15 New York Declaration for Refugees and Migrants, UN General Assembly Resolution of 19 September 2016, A/71/L. 1.

devastating disasters, but also of the gradual degradation of the environment in the context of the aforementioned slow violence[16].

In particular, climate change-induced migration is often closely linked to the depletion of natural resources, of which women are the primary users[17]. This does not stem from biological differences between women and men, but the social, economic, and political barriers that women continue to face, especially in poorer societies. For example, in countries where women are primarily responsible for water collection, they bear the brunt of the effects of climate change and may therefore be forced migrate to another country or relocate within the same country.

In some cases, however, women are even denied the right to migrate during such events, because discriminatory laws and prevailing gender stereotypes place them in a subordinate position in society, to the extent that they risk becoming the main victims, both directly and indirectly, of natural disasters.

Nevertheless, these examples call for an interpretation of the phenomenon that does not automatically place women in the category of "vulnerable people" (indeed, doubly vulnerable), but rather one that is able to grasp the complexity of intersectional forms of discrimination and the context in which they occur.

Indeed, the gender approach is almost completely absent from international treaty law on migration. Without claiming to be exhaustive, suffice it to point out that the 1951 UN Convention on the Status of Refugees defines "refugee" in an seemingly neutral way, but is conceived by reproducing legal categories of persecution that reflect male experiences[18].

In this respect, it is easy to see how the aforementioned Convention, which dates back to the immediate post-war period, was unable to respond to cases of

---

16 R. Nixon, *Slow Violence and the Environmentalism of the Poor*. Boston, 2011.

17 Although not specifically addressing the situation of displaced women, it is appropriate to recall the 2020 Special Rapporteur's report on the Human Rights of Internally Displaced Persons (SRIDP), which highlighted the "particular challenges" that displaced people face "in the context of the *slow-onset* adverse effects of climate change".

18 Iermano A. (2021). Donne migranti vittime di violenza domestica: l'interpretazione "gender-sensitive" dei giudici nazionali in conformità alla Convenzione di Istanbul. *Ordine Internazionale e Diritti Umani*, 2021, n. 3, pp. 731–753, which points out that the Geneva Convention, like other international treaties, was drafted from a "male perspective". However, the gender-sensitive interpretation provided for in the Istanbul Convention (Art. 60(2)) allows applications for international protection to be accepted in cases previously considered irrelevant, in particular in cases of domestic violence. It is therefore up to the actors of the law – first and foremost the national courts – to interpret and apply the rules from a gender perspective that is constantly "updated" and capable of responding to the social demands of the time and place.

refugee status claims based on gender-based violence as a form of persecution[19]. However, the absence of a gender dimension is not only due to the socio-political context in which the negotiations took place, but also the strong opposition between the public and private spheres that was entrenched at the time, whereby the State was not subject to international legal obligations with regard to the so-called "private" dimension of violence[20].

In fact, women's rights and the recognition of gender discrimination did not emerge until the 1970s with the adoption of the Convention on the Elimination of All Forms of Discrimination against Women (CEDAW) in 1979, and the subsequent General Recommendation No. 19 of the Committee established by CEDAW, which brought violence against women within the scope of UN law. Nonetheless, the gender dimension has been reclaimed through international soft law instruments, such as the UNHCR Gender Guidelines of 2022[21], which refer to women as an example of a "social subset defined by innate and immutable characteristics [..] and who are frequently treated differently than men"[22].

---

19 Of note is the judgment of the Court of Justice, Grand Chamber, of 16 January 2024 in Case C-621/21, *WS v. Intervyuirasht organ na Darzhavna agentsia za bezhantsite pri Ministerskia savet,* where it was held that membership of a "particular social group" on the basis of conditions in the country of origin may be considered a "reason for persecution" which may lead to recognition of refugee status, both for women in that country as a whole and for smaller groups of women who share an additional common characteristic. This is how the Court interpreted Art. 10, para. 1(d) of the Qualifications Directive (Directive 2011/95/EU).

20 Before, women were absent and invisible in the international arena, relegated to the private dimension, and therefore their activities could not acquire the character of "politics", traditionally understood as a male experience and therefore also protected by international law. On the "public-private divide", see, without claiming to be exhaustive, C. Romany (1994). State Responsibility Goes Private: A Feminist Critique of the Public/Private Distinction in International Human Rights Law. In R. Cook (ed.), *Human Rights of Women*. Philadelphia; D. Sullivan (1995). The Public/Private Distinction in International Human Rights Law. In J. Peters, A. Wolper (eds.), *Women's Rights, Human Rights: International Feminist Perspectives*. New York.

21 UNHCR, *Gender-Related Persecution within the Context of Article 1A(2) of the 1951 Convention and/or its 1967 Protocol relating to the Status of Refugees,* HCR/GIP/02/01 7 May 2002 (*Gender Guidelines*). Previously, in 1991, the UNHCR adopted the *Guidelines on the Protection of Refugee Women* (UNHCR), followed by specific guidelines on sexual violence against refugees in 1995.

22 *Gender Guidelines*, op. cit., par. 30.

On the non-neutrality of the impact of climate change and its consequences, *inter alia*, on "women's health": From CEDAW Recommendation 38 to the report of the UN Special Rapporteur on gender-based violence

To refute the supposed neutrality of climate change, it should be noted that, like the other forms of slow violence mentioned, it is a human, social, and environmental phenomenon that produces more pronounced effects by aggravating situations of vulnerability that can be exacerbated by climate change itself.

This can lead to the question of inadequate respect for human rights for all,[23] and especially for those whose human rights are already partially restricted[24], such as those living in third world[25] countries and especially women.

Some UN bodies have already spoken out on the impact of climate change on women[26]. For example, in its General Recommendation No. 37 (2018) on the gender dimension of disaster risk reduction and climate change, the CEDAW Committee emphasized that structural inequalities against women make them more vulnerable to disaster-related risks and, as is well known, to the loss of their livelihoods[27]. In particular, mortality and morbidity rates are higher among women in disaster situations as a result of their already precarious living

---

23 From a case-law point of view: United Nations Human Rights Committee (HRC), *Ioane Teitiota v. New Zealand*, CCPR/C/127/D/2928/2016 (advance unedited version), 7 January 2020. This decision has contributed to an important development, as it confirmed that the effects of climate change may, in extreme cases, cause a significant threat to an individual's right to life (the right to life in this case was based on Art. 6 of the UN International Covenant on Civil and Political Rights (ICCPR) of 16 December 1966, text in UN Treaty Series vol. 999, p. 171). In the case of the Association of Older Women against Switzerland (ric. n. 53600/20, *Verein KlimaSeniorinnen Schweiz and others v. Switzerland*, assigned to the Grand Chamber on 29 April 2022), it was argued that the right to health of women, in particular older women (in this case over 75 years of age), is in danger of being affected by rising temperatures to a greater extent than that of men.

24 S. Atrey (2023). The Inequality of Climate Change and the Difference it Makes. In C. Albertyn, H. Alviar García, M. Campbell, S. Fredman, M. Rodriguez de Assis Machado (eds.), *Feminist Frontiers*. Edward Elgar, p. 18.

25 On this point, see for example, UNCTAD (2022). *The Least Developed Countries Report 2022*, https://unctad.org/system/files/official-document/ldc2022_en.pdf, p. 3 ss.

26 The term "women" in this paragraph includes, where relevant, adolescents and girls.

27 CEDAW Committee, General Recommendation No. 37 (GR 37) on the gender dimension of disaster risk reduction in the context of climate change, 13 March 2018, CEDAW/C/GC/37, par. 3.

conditions (e.g. restricted access to health care, water, food), but also as a result of response mechanisms to environmental emergencies that do not take into account the specific needs of different groups of women[28].

In addition, gender-based violence against women, including sexual violence, which is prevalent in humanitarian crises, is exacerbated in disaster situations and by the destruction of resources[29]. Access to education, already limited for girls due to social, cultural, and economic barriers, is further complicated after disasters due to the destruction of infrastructure, lack of teachers, and economic hardship[30]. In terms of the right to work and social protection, inequalities between women (often in precarious and informal employment) and men are exacerbated. The burden of domestic and care work increases after disasters due to the destruction of food stocks, housing, and infrastructure, including water and energy supplies[31].

Women's right to health is disproportionately affected by disasters and climate change, always because of structural inequalities in society, particularly access to food, health, and care[32].

It is not surprising that the CEDAW[33] Committee has focussed on access to health services and reproductive health[34], although it does not mention that, for

---

28 Ibid., par. 4.
29 Ibid., pars. 55 and 56.
30 Ibid., par. 58–59.
31 Ibid., par. 61–62.
32 Par. 66.
33 In CEDAW, the protection of the right to health is enshrined in both Art. 12, which provides for women's equal access to medical care, family planning services and appropriate care for pregnancy, maternity and breastfeeding, as well as in Art. 10 with regard to the necessary information on family planning practices, that Art. 11 with regard to the protection of women's work, in which "the protection of health and safety in working conditions, including the safeguarding of the functioning of reproduction", in addition to Art. 10, is to be guaranteed. The Committee on the Environment, Public Health and Consumer Protection, on the health of "rural women", to provide them with adequate access to health care, including information, assistance and services related to family planning. This is due to the fact that women living in rural areas often face multiple difficulties in using contraceptives, including emergency contraception, due to the lack of geographically accessible pharmacies, and therefore do not have the opportunity to decide freely and responsibly on the number of their children.
34 The protection of women's reproductive health is particularly important within CEDAW, as it is the only human rights treaty that affirms women's rights in the area of reproduction. The aim of the Convention is to eliminate discrimination on the basis of sex, even if it is based on cultural practices in certain countries. See, C. Bustelo (1995). Reproductive Health and CEDAW. *The American University Law Review*, 1995, p. 1145.

example, high levels of pollution caused by certain substances, including mercury, have a significant impact on women's reproductive rights[35].

Furthermore, the World Health Organization considers migration as an independent risk factor of HIV among women[36], noting serious mental health problems among migrant women who are victims of environmental disasters, extreme poverty, religious, racial, ethnic persecution, among others.

Moreover, migrant women, especially those living in rural areas, are directly affected by the effects of climate change, resulting in reduced food security and land degradation. In many areas, even though they have no legal title to land ownership, they are left solely responsible for agricultural activities as the male segment of society migrates[37]. Violence can also occur through human trafficking in the field, at the border, and in the destination country[38].

In applying CEDAW to disaster risk reduction and climate change, the Committee has emphasised three general principles of the legal instrument: equality and non-discrimination; participation and empowerment; and access to justice[39]. Despite the important step forward in considering environmental issues as a matter of inequality under CEDAW, the Committee focuses on disaster management, particularly mitigation and adaptation, but refrains from considering the "inevitability of climate change" and adopting a "more radical and transformative approach"[40].

The United Nations Commission on the *Status* of Women[41], at its 66th session from 14 to 25 March 2022, also identified its priority theme as "achieving gender equality and the empowerment of all women and girls in the context of climate change, environmental and disaster risk reduction policies and programmes".

In its conclusions of 29 March 2022, the Commission reiterated the disproportionate impact of climate change, environmental degradation, and disasters

---

35 See note 19 on the Minamata example.

36 UNAIDS, *The Gap Report*, 2014.

37 Ibid., par. 70.

38 Ibid., par. 75.

39 Ibid., par. 26. See also, S. De Vido, E. Fornalé (2023). Achievements and Hurdles Towards Women's Access to Climate Justice. In E. Fornalé, F. Cristani (eds.), *Women's Empowerment and its Limits*, Springer.

40 S. Atrey, *The Inequality*, op. cit., p. 35.

41 The status of women and the advancement of their rights have long been a focus of the United Nations, and it is no coincidence that the 2030 Agenda for Sustainable Development includes gender equality among the 17 goals to be achieved by 2030 (A/RES/70/1 of 25 September 2015, p. 10).

on women, but also stressed the importance of recognizing the role of women as agents of change (women's *agency*)[42].

It further stressed that women face "specific challenges" in the context of displacement caused by climate change and environmental degradation, including increased risk of violence, reduced access to work, education, basic health services, including reproductive health services, and psychosocial support[43].

With specific regard to migration, the Commission underlined, *inter alia*, the importance of recognizing the positive contribution of migrant women, promoting a gender perspective in migration policies and programmes, responding to the vulnerabilities they face, and addressing all forms of violence that may occur as a result of displacement[44]. The Commission also recalled the Agenda for the Protection of Cross-Border Displaced Persons in the Context of Disasters and Climate Change, and the Platform on Disaster Displacement[45].

A few months later, in July 2022, Reem Alsalem, the Special Rapporteur on violence against women[46], its causes, and consequences, published a report on violence against women in the context of the climate crisis, including environmental degradation, related responses, and disaster risk reduction[47]. The very title of the report makes the link between climate change and other forms of slow violence more explicit than the CEDAW recommendation, which merely extends the same observations made on climate change to forms of environmental degradation[48]. The Special Rapporteur noted, "The combined impacts of sudden-onset natural disasters and slow-onset events, environmental degradation and forced displacement seriously affect women's and girls' rights to life,

---

42 UN Commission on the status of women (2022). *Achieving gender equality and the empowerment of all women and girls in the context of climate change, environmental and disaster risk reduction policies and programmes, Agreed conclusions*, 66th session, E/CN.6/2022/L.7, par. 22.

43 Ibid.

44 Ibid., par. 60.

45 Ibid., Recommendation (r).

46 Special Rapporteur on violence against women and girls, its causes and consequences (UNSRVAW), Reem Alsalem, *Violence against Women and Girls in the Context of the Climate Crisis, including Environmental Degradation and Related Disaster Risk Mitigation and Response*, A/77/136, 11 July 2022. UN Special Rapporteur on Violence against Women, its Causes and Consequences of 11 July 2022.

47 A/77/136, cit.

48 GR 37, par. 13.

access to food and nutrition, safe drinking water and sanitation, education and training, adequate housing, land, decent work and labour protection"[49].

The report highlights how climate change exposes those affected, especially women, to human rights violations that constitute forms of violence and persecution that may qualify them for refugee status[50]. As a result of intersectional elements of discrimination, the category of women at risk must also include those who defend, preserve, and denounce the state of resources and ecosystems: human rights defenders (women's rights and environmental rights).

The phenomenon of migration and internal displacement emerges at various points in the Special Rapporteur's analysis. For example, the report highlights that the likelihood of violence is multiplied when women are displaced or in emergency shelters[51], when they migrate to countries, cities, and peri-urban areas as a result of forced displacement or planned relocation and face difficulties in accessing adequate housing, work, social protection mechanisms[52], and when they are at risk of being trafficked for sexual exploitation or domestic labour following disasters[53].

It is evident that climate change can lead to the migration of the male segment of society, leaving women to provide for the family and to enter a labour market characterized by gender pay gaps and economic disempowerment[54]. In order to avoid forced migration or trafficking and thus escape violence, girls are forced into early marriages, which are themselves a form of gender-based violence, but are perceived by poor families as a form of protection[55].

In other cases, climate change and environmental degradation lead to the forced displacement of women, who are at high risk of violence, especially sexual violence[56]. As the Secretary General of the United Nations noted, "When women are not consulted or included in decisions on issues that have had a direct impact on their lives such as education, health, economic development or conflict resolution, the results of the policies risk being harmful and ineffective and leading to the violation of human rights". This point was reiterated by the Special

---

49 A/77/136, cit., par. 7.
50 Ibid.
51 Ibid., par. 25.
52 Ibid., par. 27.
53 This occurred, for example, in the Philippines after Typhoon Haiyan in 2013. Ibid., par. 30.
54 Ibid., par. 43–44.
55 Ibid., par. 47.
56 Ibid., par. 55

Rapporteur in the report presented in October 2022, which emphasized that the need to ensure the inclusive and equitable participation of women in decision-making bodies on climate change is a key element in remedying the progressive erosion and denigration of democratic processes. And as the Special Rapporteur repeatedly emphasized, this can only be achieving through the inclusive and equitable participation of women in decision-making bodies on climate change.

Brief concluding reflections

In light of the above, it is hoped that a binding legal framework will be established to protect the rights of "climate migrants" in general and "climate migrant women" in particular, taking into account the gender-climate nexus and its consequences, especially in terms of health.

As noted, climate change creates conditions that accentuate migration, acting as drivers and factors that compel women and girls to leave their countries of origin, disrupting their lives for the various reasons outlines.

In this context, the issue of women's access to health services, reproductive health, and psychosocial support services is undoubtedly crucial.

However, in order to move away from considering women merely as "victims" of climate change, efforts are being made at the international level – as noted above – to increase their participation in the formulation and implementation of policies and action plans to respond to climate change and disasters, to reduce the risks, and to influence the decisions in this regard.

In particular, the 2015 Paris Agreement on climate change emphasizes in its preamble the need for parties to respect, promote, and take into account the right to empowerment of women when taking action to combat climate change.

Similarly, within the European Union, the Gender Equality Strategy 2020–2025 and the actions envisaged under the European Green Deal[57], such as the EU Strategy on Adaptation to Climate Change, take into account the role of young women in driving change.

In conclusion, women are the main victims of the harmful effects of global warming, but at the same time play a key role in the fight against climate change. This implies the need to address climate change from a gender perspective at

---

57 The European Green Pact or European Green Deal is a set of policy initiatives proposed by the European Commission with the overall objective of achieving climate neutrality in Europe by 2050. On 14 July 2021, the European Commission adopted the "Fit for 55" climate package, which includes legislative proposals to achieve the objectives of the Green Deal by 2030.

both the international and European level, and define an effective and efficient response.

References

Arendt, H. (2008) [1970]. *Sulla violenza.* Parma, p. 90

Atrey, S. (2023). The inequality of climate change and the difference it makes. In C. Albertyn, H. Alviar García, M. Campbell, S. Fredman, & M. Rodriguez de Assis Machado (Eds.), *Feminist frontiers.* Edward Elgar, p. 18.

Bakošová, L., & Scott, M. (2020). *Climate change, disasters, and the refugee convention.* Cambridge.

Behrman, S., & Kent, A. (Eds.). (2018). *Climate refugees: Beyond the legal impasse?* Abingdon/NewYork.

Bustelo, C. (1995). Reproductive Health and CEDAW. *The American University Law Review*, 1995, p. 1145.

Cusato, E. (2021). *The ecology of war and peace.* Cambridge.

De Vido, S. (2023). In dubio pro futuris generationibus: una risposta giuridica eco-centrica alla slow violence. In M. Frulli (Ed.), *L'interesse delle future generazioni nel diritto internazionale e dell'Unione europea.* Atti del Convegno SIDI. Napoli: Editoriale Scientifica.

De Vido, S., & Fornalé, E. (2023). Achievements and hurdles towards women's access to climate justice. In E. Fornalé & F. Cristani (Eds.), *Women's empowerment and its limits.* Springer.

Fornalé, E. (2024). Parità di genere e cambiamenti climatici in tempi di "polycrisis". In A. Di Stasi (Ed.), *Dalla non discriminazione alle pari opportunità. Un itinerario di confronto, ricerca e sperimentazione di buone prassi a UNISA… e oltre. Atti del Convegno internazionale di studi tenuto in occasione della Giornata internazionale della donna 2023.* Milano: Ledizioni, p. 117 ss.

Gaard, G. (1993). Living interconnections with animals and nature. In G. Gaard (Ed.), *Ecofeminism. Women, animals, nature.* Philadelphia, p. 1.

Iermano, A. (2021). Donne migranti vittime di violenza domestica: l'interpretazione "gender-sensitive" dei giudici nazionali in conformità alla Convenzione di Istanbul. *Ordine Internazionale e Diritti Umani*, n. 3, pp. 731–753.

Ionesco, D. et al. (2018). *The Atlas of environmental migration.* Abingdon/New York.

Lama, P., Hamza, M., & Wester, M. (2021). Gendered dimensions of migration in relation to climate change. *Climate and Development*, 2021, n. 13, 4, pp. 326–336, in particular, p. 329.

McAdam, J. (Ed.). (2010). *Climate change and displacement: Multidisciplinary perspectives*. Oxford.

Mizutamari, M. (2020). Michiko Ishimure e i "popoli nomadi". *Deportate, Esuli e Profughe*. 2020, n. 41–42, pp. 125–134.

Nixon, R. (2011). *Slow violence and the environmentalism of the poor*. Boston.

Randall, A. (n.d.). *Climate refugees: How many are there? How many will there be?*, available at the link http://climatemigration.org.uk/climate-refugees-how-many/

Romany, C. (1994). State responsibility goes private: A feminist critique of the public/private distinction in International Human Rights Law. In R. Cook (Ed.), *Human rights of women*. Philadelphia.

Sciaccaluga, G. (2020). *International Law and the protection of climate refugees*. Cham.

Special Rapporteur on violence against women and girls, its causes and consequences (UNSRVAW), Reem Alsalem. (2022). *Violence against Women and Girls in the Context of the Climate Crisis, including Environmental Degradation and Related Disaster Risk Mitigation and Response*, A/77/136, 11 July 2022.

Sullivan, D. (1995). The public/private distinction in International Human Rights Law. In J. Peters, & A. Wolper (Eds.), *Women's rights, human rights: International feminist perspectives*. New York.

Tonolo, S., & Monego, D. (2023). Il diritto alla salute delle donne migranti: garanzie costituzionali e internazionali a confronto. In A. Di stasi, R. Cadin, A. Iermano, & V. Zambrano (Eds.), *Donne migranti e violenza di genere nel contesto giuridico internazionale ed europeo/Migrant women and gender-based violence in the international and european legal framework*. Napoli: Editoriale Scientifica, p. 371 ss.

Zorzi Giustiniani, F. (2021). *International Law in disaster scenarios – Applicable rules and principles*. Cham.

Simona Gaudi and Sara Mellano

Epigenetics of violence against women: From molecular scars to precision prevention

Abstract: Violence against women is a structural and not a contingent problem, a complex and widespread phenomenon in all social classes globally. The relevance that gender-based violence continues to have in our daily lives requires an innovative and intersectoral vision to limit its physical and psychological consequences on women's health. Among the psychiatric disorders, the post-traumatic stress disorder is the most prevalent with highly disabling consequences that remain for a long time and are reflected in a decrease in expectation and quality of life. The problem is complex and has several facets that require the integration of molecular research with rigorous statistical analysis and with social, educational, clinical and care interventions. In this contribution, we address the major challenges in the interaction between genome and violence against women, one of the future developments of precision medicine. A growing body of research has shown that violence can affect the functionality of our genome through epigenetic modifications and that epigenetic scars identification can provide specific therapeutic targets for precision prevention interventions. The Epigenetic for WomEn (EpiWE) multicentric project provides the unique opportunity to collect the DNA samples of women who have suffered violence, in a dedicated biobank for the identification of epigenetic molecular pathways associated to the onset of chronic and noncommunicable diseases

Introduction

Violence against women is a major global public health problem and a violation of human rights. This plague runs across all social classes and ethnicity, and it is associated with a considerable negative influence on women's health and behaviour worldwide. The United Nations defines violence against women as "any act of gender-based violence that results in or is likely to result in, physical, sexual, or mental harm or suffering to women, including threats to such acts, coercion or arbitrary deprivation of liberty, whether occurring in public or in private life" (United Nation, 1993). The World Health Organization reports that about 30 % of women have experienced worldwide some form of violence, with serious consequences on physical and psychological health (WHO, 2013). In Italy, the National Institute of Statistics data reveal that 31.5 % of women, aged between 16 and 70, have experienced some form of physical or sexual violence during their life (Istat, 2014; 2022). From a health perspective, women who experience gender-based violence tend to face health issues more frequently compared to those who do not encounter such violence. Among all forms of violence against women, intimate partner violence (IPV) is the most prevalent. The IPV definition, provided by the Centers for Disease Control and Prevention (CDC), includes physical violence, sexual violence, stalking, and psychological aggression perpetrated by a current or former intimate partner (CDC, 2021). IPV destroys women's feelings of love, trust, and self-esteem, with important negative consequences on physical and psychological health (Khan, 2016). Violence, both physical and psychological, can have a lasting impact on the mental and physical health of victims. Apart from the individual and non-refundable costs incurred by IPV victims, which include premature death, pain and suffering, the costs of violence against women are spread throughout society.

Survivors' health outcomes

The relationship between stressful factors and an individual health or illness condition is a complex and multifaceted one. Stress, in general, is known to have a profound impact on both mental and physical well-being. When stress is prolonged or intense, as in the case of IPV, it can lead to a range of negative health outcomes. The health consequences of gender-based violence can be immediate and direct (physical injuries), or indirect, medium- or long-term (chronic diseases, psychiatric disorders) and more difficult to correlate directly to violence

Scientific literature reports that IPV survivors commonly suffer from various consequences that range from higher morbidity and mortality and physical and psychological health problems (Cirici Amell et al., 2023). There is a well-documented link between gender-based violence and long-term health issues, including chronic and psychosomatic diseases, cardiovascular disorders, chronic pelvic or abdominal pain, and psychiatric disorders. The latter are particularly challenging to directly attribute to the experienced violence, often resulting in significantly adverse effects on women's health and overall quality of life. (Resnick et al., 1997; Campbell, 2002).

Although these are less obvious and often difficult to diagnose health conditions, there is a consistent and growing body of research on the associations between IPV and women mental health problems. In particular depression and PTSD appear to be influenced by multiple factors, such as the type, duration, and severity of violence (Stewart & Vigod, 2019). PTSD symptoms may include severe anxiety, flashbacks, nightmares, symptoms of increased arousal such as irritability or anger, or symptoms included persistent avoidance of trauma-related situations (Castro-Vale & Carvalho, 2020). Following DSM-V criteria, PTSD symptoms must last for more than a month, so the evaluation of victims of sexual violence has been postponed (at least one month) after the acute traumatic event to meet DSM-V criteria. The 11th edition of the International Classification of Diseases (ICD) by the World Health Organization (WHO, 2022) has incorporated a novel condition known as complex post-traumatic stress disorder (complex PTSD), supplementing post-traumatic stress disorder (PTSD) within the overarching category labelled "Disorders specifically associated with stress". Both disorders necessitate exposure to a traumatic event for consideration. Complex PTSD diagnosis encompasses these three PTSD clusters along with three additional symptom clusters, which indicate pervasive and chronic disruptions in self-organization. These include affect dysregulation, an extremely negative self-concept, and challenges in forming and sustaining relationships.

As illustrated in the passages above, intimate partner violence (IPV) and gender-based violence (GBV) can lead to a broad spectrum of mental health effects for the victims, varying in intensity from mild to severe.

A better understanding of the complex interplay of biological, psychological, social, and cultural factors involved is essential for developing effective prevention strategies, providing appropriate support for survivors, and fostering a broader societal shift toward ending gender-based violence.

Epigenetics and PTSD

Violence, as a negative "socio-environmental" factor can influence and modify the functionality of our genome through epigenetic modifications, significantly contributing to the onset of chronic and non-communicable diseases. With the term epigenetics, we indicate the changes that occur on the DNA and that affect its expression, without altering its sequence (Greenberg & Bourc'his, 2019). In fact, the DNA sequence remains unchanged, but the addition of chemical groups or small molecules in specific locations turn on or off gene expression. Epigenetics is a relatively young pursuit in the biological sciences and this fundamental knowledge is now being integrated with the environmental factors in complex disease determination (Zhang et al., 2020a).

Understanding the interplay between genetics and the environment is essential for unraveling the complexity of PTSD susceptibility and resilience. The correlation between PTSD and epigenetic modifications is all now being studied concerning various categories of subjects such as war veterans, abused children and holocaust survivors (Yehuda et al., 2014). Research approaches should therefore include epigenome analysis in people exposed to both acute and chronic violence, as well as studies on animal models to identify underlying molecular mechanisms. In this context, genome-violence interaction is a promising field of research with wide implications for understanding chronic and noncommunicable diseases. However, only recently scientists have begun to examine how violence can affect the epigenome and, as a result, the susceptibility to disease. So far, findings have been mostly anecdotal and most epidemiological studies on gender-based violence focus on short-term effects, while long-term ones are neglected or marginally included even though they consist of serious and complex consequences. Long-term morbidity and PTSD are due, among other things, to the influence of traumatic stress on the physiological functioning of the so-called hypothalamic-pituitary-adrenal axis, a key system involved in the body's stress response. Epigenetic modifications may contribute to this dysregulation by influencing the expression of genes involved in the HPA axis, potentially perpetuating a cycle of stress-related symptoms.

The remarkable growth in understanding epigenetic mechanisms and the impact of epigenetics on contemporary biology has added new insight into the molecular processes that connect the brain with behaviour, neuroendocrine responsiveness, and immune outcome (Mathews & Janusek, 2011).

Differentially regulated methylation levels of genes associated with Hypothalamic-pituitary-adrenal (HPA) axis, neurotransmission and inflammation genes were found to be linked to PTSD (Rusiecki et al., 2012; Smith et al., 2020). The results of epigenetic programming and reprogramming in the domain of emotions, positive and/or negative, could affect a relatively new domain of epigenetics of IPV and PTSD (Gaudi et al., 2016). PTSD is multigenic and multifactorial psychiatric diseases, with a complex and largely unknown genetic architecture with a significant social cost. The research in the interaction between genome activity and the impact of violence against women on the individual psyche is certainly one of the most promising areas for the future of psychiatry. Epigenetics is the molecular mechanism that connects society to biology, humanities and social sciences to life sciences. Here, we address the major challenges and opportunities facing the interaction of the genome with violence against women, the Epigenetic for WomEn (EpiWE) project.

EpiWE project, preliminary results

We are rapidly advancing upon the post genomic era in which genetic/epigenetic information will have to be examined in multiple health care situations in attempt to offer a better life of patients. In the "Epigenetics for WomEn" (EpiWE) study, we investigated the epigenetic markers in 62 women exposed to violence and 50 women with no history of violence, recruited at the Service for Sexual and Domestic Violence (Policlinico, University of Milan). All women aged 18–65, who signed the informed consent, were monitored for their physical and psychological conditions. Violence screening procedures were already validated in the Emergency Department (ED), according to the European Injury Database specifications, by an anti-violence team, oriented to early listening of the patient and avoiding the development of chronic physical and psychological pathologies. A follow-up procedure is implemented at 6, 12 and 18 months from the hospital discharge. The questionnaire evaluated the severity of the suffered violence, its risks of recurrence and escalation, the personal and context vulnerabilities of the victim, the state of psychological and physical health on standardized scales. Blood samples were collected, and DNAs were extracted and underwent the epigenetic analysis of 10 stress-related genes: *ADCYAP1*, *BDNF*, *CRHR1*, *DRD2*, *FKBP*, *IGF2*, *LSD1*, *NR3C1*, *PRTFDC1* and *SLC6A4* (Piccinini et al., 2023). Quantitative methylation evaluation of these ten selected trauma/stress-related genes revealed the differential iper-methylation in the promoter of three gene: brain-derived neurotrophic factor (BDNF), dopamine receptor D2 (DRD2) and insulin-like growth factor 2 (IGF2). The Brain-Derived Neurotrophic Factor (BDNF) gene encodes a neurotrophic factor derived from the brain, one of the major regulators of synaptic transmission and neuroplasticity, already involved in stress response, learning and memory (Gray et al., 2013). Studies in rats have shown that physical activity induces hypomethylation of the promoter with a consequent increase and resumption of gene expression (Gomez-Pinilla et al., 2011), suggesting that the BDNF gene promoter may be an adjustable target for gene expression. In the case of Kim study, war veterans with PTSD show similar results of BDNF gene hypermethylation (Kim et al., 2017). The DRD2 gene encodes a protein that is important for memory formation and neuronal plasticity and has been associated in veterans with severe comorbidities in PTSD sufferers (Lawford et al., 2006). In a recent study of health workers who faced the SARS-CoV-2 pandemic in the forefront, hypermethylation in the neurotransmission-associated DRD2 gene was also highlighted (Tabano et al., 2022). DRD2 hypermethylation was also measured in the DNA of girls who had been abused during childhood, indicating how chronic psychological stress can lead to depression and the development of PTSD (Christensen et al., 2021). The Insulin Growth Factor 2 gene, IGF2 codifies for the factor 2 of insulinic growth considered an important gene for the fetal development and for the placenta, that are regulated by genomic imprinting (Tabano et al., 2010). In addition, IGF2 plays an important role in memory building, in several psychiatric diseases and autism, and could be considered a good candidate for developing new pharmacological treatments for neurological and psychiatric diseases (Pardo et al., 2019; Mills et al., 2007). Animal models studies have shown how treatments with IGF2 are able to increase the functions of memory, regression in cognitive deterioration, motor deficit and seizures (Yu et al., 2020; Cruz et al., 2020). In mice, intracerebral injections of the IGF2 protein have been shown to induce increased BDNF levels in the hippocampus, suggesting a common molecular pathway between the two IGF2 and BDNF genes (Mellott et al., 2014). These findings, although preliminary, are promising in revealing epigenetic markers in genes mediators of brain plasticity, which can modulate learning and memory in response to stress associated with intimate partner and sexual violence-induced PTSD. These preliminary results could be useful for the implementation of prevention strategies also to avoid any long-term effects. Prolonged stress caused by gender violence leads to activation of allostatic systems with serious consequences on the state of health. Understanding and identifying the epigenetic modifications that relates to violence against women, is important because of their reversibility. To be able to identify the molecular mechanisms behind the onset of PTSD in the context of violence, could highlight the origin of the disease and identify innovative strategies to increase resilience. EpiWE focuses on the early identification of epigenetic scars and on limiting the long-term consequences of violence. The epigenetic/epigenomic health profile represents the first step for precision prevention. Chronic, disabling and non-communicable diseases often occur many years after the violence and even from a legal point of view, the link between trauma and the onset of pathology is denied. Analysis of epigenetic markers could provide us important information about the violence-induced epigenetic pathways that accelerate ageing and trigger molecular processes that bring out early chronic and invalidating diseases. In recent years, numerous scientific studies have shown that chronic stress promotes the development and progression of female cancers, particularly those of the ovary and breast and therefore it would be essential to identify early molecular markers to counteract the onset of such diseases (Obradović et al., 2019). The epigenetic markers studied so far and those that will be further studied on the entire genome, will allow to diachronically bind the pathological consequences of violence.

Multicenter project and ViVa biobank

The natural evolution of the EpiWE project is the realization of a multicentric project throughout the country. The involvement of other centers allows to increase the number of patient samples and to evaluate in a follow-up study, the possible variation of the epigenomic profile (epigenetic markers on the entire genome) of patients. The epigenomic profile could reveal new epigenetic scars involved in other biological pathways related to the long-term health effects of violence (e.g. cancer, cardiovascular and autoimmune diseases). All biological samples will be accompanied by a series of data on psychophysical well-being, focussing on the stress related pathologies. The investigation of the epigenetic marker role in parallel with psycho-physical health data could elucidate the correlation with pathways not yet well identified and that could be traced back to the susceptibility to other non-communicable diseases. In fact, scientific evidence shows that domestic violence, by inducing chronic stress in victims, can promote the development of tumors not only during the period of stress, but also in the following years (Zhang et al., 2020b; Hong et al., 2021). In the long term, this approach would optimize treatment, improve the quality of life of victims and provides more objective damage characterization in medical-legal prospects. The multicentric epigenetic study and the establishment of the ViVa biobank within the Italian National Institute of Health, will provide the first large collection of biological samples dedicated to violence against women. ViVa biobank has dedicated areas equipped with advanced technologies that allow to prepare, analyse and store the samples and their data. In parallel, ViVa ensures the highest standards of environmental sustainability, through intelligent management technologies and the use of renewable energy that help reduce the environmental impact of the structure. This prospective study represents innovative and unique solutions for approaching violence against women by precision medicine strategies to ensure women a healthier life. The molecular mechanisms behind the onset of stress-related diseases in the context of violence against women could highlight the origin of the disease and promote innovative strategies for limiting the long-term negative effects. Precision prevention protocols will represent an important advantage for tailoring specific health strategies and reducing the prevalence of non-communicable diseases associate to violence against women. To fully understand genome-violence interaction, multidisciplinary research involving genetics, neurobiology, psychology, and medicine is required. The importance of the interconnection of emergency flows and hospital discharge forms, through the individual code of the patient, should also be accompanied by initiatives that offer women long-term health care. The costs of violence are enormous, and only through precise prevention we can achieve a better future for women, children and society, as a whole. Understanding how violence affects the epigenome could lead to new interventions for victims of violence in a personalized medicine perspective and could help prevent the long-term consequences on mental and physical health. A better understanding of the real consequences of violence, the implementation of prevention information campaigns that tend to improve the lives of surviving women could lead to considerable cost savings on the National Health Service.

Acknowledgments: We would like to thank all the women who have and will participate in the EpiWE study, the colleagues without whom this work would not have been possible: Piccinini A, Bailo P, Barbara G, Bertuccio P, La Vecchia C, Kustermann A, Falzano L and Costabile E.

Conflicts of Interest: The authors declared no potential conflicts of interest with respect to the research, authorship, and/or publication of this article.

References

Campbell, J. C. (2002). Health consequences of intimate partner violence. *The Lancet, 359*(9314), 1331–1336. https://doi.org/10.1016/s0140-6736(02)08336-8

Castro-Vale, I., & Carvalho, D. (2020). The pathways between cortisol-related regulation genes and PTSD psychotherapy. *Healthcare, 8*(4), 376. https://doi.org/10.3390/healthcare8040376

CDC Centers for Disease Control and Prevention. (2021, October 11). *Fast Facts: Preventing Intimate Partner Violence.* Centers for Disease Control and Prevention. Retrieved January 8, 2024, from https://www.cdc.gov/violenceprevention/intimatepartnerviolence/fastfact.html

Christensen, J., Beveridge, J. K., Wang, M., Orr, S. L., Noel, M., & Mychasiuk, R. (2021). A Pilot Study Investigating the Role of Gender in the Intergenerational Relationships between Gene Expression, Chronic Pain, and Adverse Childhood Experiences in a Clinical Sample of Youth with Chronic Pain. *Epigenomes, 5*(2), 9. https://doi.org/10.3390/epigenomes5020009

Cirici Amell, R., Soler, A. R., Cobo, J., & Soldevilla Alberti, J. M. (2023). Psychological consequences and daily life adjustment for victims of intimate partner violence. *International Journal of Psychiatry in Medicine, 58*(1), 6–19. https://doi.org/10.1177/00912174211050504

Cruz, E., Descalzi, G., Steinmetz, A. B., Scharfman, H. E., Katzman, A., & Alberini, C. M. (2020). CIM6P/IGF-2 receptor ligands reverse Deficits in Angelman Syndrome model Mice. *Autism Research, 14*(1), 29–45. https://doi.org/10.1002/aur.2418

Gaudi, S., Guffanti, G., Fallon, J., & Macciardi, F. (2016). Epigenetic mechanisms and associated brain circuits in the regulation of positive emotions: A role for transposable elements. *The Journal of comparative neurology, 524*(15), 2944–2954. https://doi.org/10.1002/cne.24046

Gomez-Pinilla, F., Zhuang, Y., Feng, J., Ying, Z., & Fan, G. (2011). Exercise impacts brain-derived neurotrophic factor plasticity by engaging mechanisms of epigenetic regulation. *European Journal of Neuroscience, 33*(3), 383–390. https://doi.org/10.1111/j.1460-9568.2010.07508

Greenberg, M. V. C., & Bourc'his, D. (2019). The diverse roles of DNA methylation in mammalian development and disease. *Nature Reviews. Molecular Cell Biology, 20*(10), 590–607. https://doi.org/10.1038/s41580-019-0159-6

Gray, J. D., Milner, T. A., & McEwen, B. S. (2013). Dynamic plasticity: The role of glucocorticoids, brain-derived neurotrophic factor and other trophic factors. *Neuroscience, 239*, 214–227. https://doi.org/10.1016/j.neuroscience.2012.08.034

Hong, H., Ji, M., & Lai, D. (2021). Chronic stress effects on tumor: Pathway and mechanism. *Frontiers in Oncology, 11.* https://doi.org/10.3389/fonc.2021.738252

Istat. (2014). *Violenza sulle donne.* Istat. Retrieved January 9, 2024, from https://www.istat.it/it/violenza-sulle-donne/il-fenomeno/violenza-dentro-e-fuori-la-famiglia/numero-delle-vittime-e-forme-di-violenza#:~:text=Il%20 31%2C5%25%20delle%2016,della%20violenza%20sessuale%20come%20lo

Istat. (2022). *La violenza sulle donne.* Istat. Retrieved January 9, 2024, from https://www.istat.it/it/violenza-sulle-donne

Khan, K. S. (2016). BJOG Editor's choice: Intimate partner violence destroys love like tears blur clear vision. *BJOG: An International Journal of Obstetrics and Gynaecology, 123*(8), 1249. https://doi.org/10.1111/1471-0528.13664

Kim, T. Y., Kim, S. J., Chung, H. G., Choi, J. H., Kim, S. H., & Kang, J. I. (2017). Epigenetic alterations of the BDNF gene in combat-related post-traumatic stress disorder. *Acta psychiatrica Scandinavica, 135*(2), 170–179. https://doi.org/10.1111/acps.12675

Lawford, B. R., Young, R., Noble, E. P., Kann, B., & Ritchie, T. (2006). The D2 dopamine receptor (DRD2) gene is associated with co-morbid depression, anxiety and social dysfunction in untreated veterans with post-traumatic stress disorder. *European psychiatry: the journal of the Association of European Psychiatrists, 21*(3), 180–185. https://doi.org/10.1016/j.eurpsy.2005.01.006

Mathews, H. L., & Janusek, L. W. (2011). Epigenetics and psychoneuroimmunology: mechanisms and models. *Brain, Behavior, and Immunity, 25*(1), 25–39. https://doi.org/10.1016/j.bbi.2010.08.009

Mellott, T. J., Pender, S., Burke, R. M., Langley, E. A., & Blusztajn, J. K. (2014). IGF2 ameliorates amyloidosis, increases cholinergic marker expression and raises

BMP9 and neurotrophin levels in the hippocampus of the APPSWEPS1DE9 Alzheimer's Disease model mice. *PLOS ONE, 9*(4), e94287. https://doi.org/10.1371/journal.pone.0094287

Mills, J. F., Kroner, D. G., & Hemmati, T. (2007). The validity of violence risk estimates: An issue of item performance. *Psychological Services, 4*(1), 1–12. https://doi.org/10.1037/1541-1559.4.1.1

Obradović, M., Hamelin, B., Manevski, N., Couto, J., Sethi, A., Coissieux, M., Münst, S., Okamoto, R., Kohler, H., Schmidt, A., & Bentires-Alj, M. (2019). Glucocorticoids promote breast cancer metastasis. *Nature, 567*(7749), 540–544. https://doi.org/10.1038/s41586-019-1019-4

Pardo, M., Cheng, Y., Sitbon, Y. H., Lowell, J. A., Grieco, S. F., Worthen, R. J., Desse, S., & Barreda-Diaz, A. (2019). Insulin growth factor 2 (IGF2) as an emergent target in psychiatric and neurological disorders. Review. *Neuroscience Research, 149*, 1–13. https://doi.org/10.1016/j.neures.2018.10.012

Piccinini, A., Bailo, P., Barbara, G., Miozzo, M., Tabano, S., Colapietro, P., Farè, C., Sirchia, S. M., Battaglioli, E., Bertuccio, P., Manenti, G., Micci, L., La Vecchia, C., Kustermann, A., & Gaudi, S. (2023). Violence against women and stress-related disorders: Seeking for associated epigenetic signatures, a pilot study. *Healthcare, 11*(2), 173. https://doi.org/10.3390/healthcare11020173

Resnick, H. S., Acierno, R., & Kilpatrick, D. G. (1997). Health impact of interpersonal violence. 2: Medical and mental health outcomes. *Behavioral medicine, 23*(2), 65–78. https://doi.org/10.1080/08964289709596730

Rusiecki, J., Chen, L., Srikantan, V., Zhang, L., Yan, L., Polin, M. L., & Baccarelli, A. (2012). DNA methylation in repetitive elements and post-traumatic stress disorder: a case–control study of US military service members. *Epigenomics, 4*(1), 29–40. https://doi.org/10.2217/epi.11.116

Smith, A. K., Ratanatharathorn, A., Maihofer, A. X., Naviaux, R. K., Aiello, A. E., Amstadter, A. B., Ashley-Koch, A. E., Baker, D. G., Beckham, J. C., Boks, M. P., Bromet, E., Dennis, M., Galea, S., Garrett, M. E., Geuze, E., Guffanti, G., Hauser, M. A., Katrinli, S., Kilaru, V., Kessler, R. C., Nievergelt, C. M. (2020). Epigenome-wide meta-analysis of PTSD across 10 military and civilian cohorts identifies methylation changes in AHRR. *Nature communications, 11*(1), 5965. https://doi.org/10.1038/s41467-020-19615-x

Stewart, D. E., & Vigod, S. N. (2019). Update on mental health aspects of intimate partner violence. *Medical Clinics of North America, 103*(4), 735–749. https://doi.org/10.1016/j.mcna.2019.02.010

Tabano, S., Colapietro, P., Cetin, I., Grati, F. R., Zanutto, S., Mandò, C., Antonazzo, P., Pileri, P., Rossella, F., Larizza, L., Sirchia, S. M., & Miozzo, M. (2010). Epigenetic modulation of theIGF2/H19imprinted domain in human embryonic and extra-embryonic compartments and its possible role in fetal growth restriction. *Epigenetics, 5*(4), 313–324. https://doi.org/10.4161/epi.5.4.11637

Tabano, S., Tassi, L., Cannone, M. G., Brescia, G., Gaudioso, G., Ferrara, M., Colapietro, P., Fontana, L., Miozzo, M., Croci, G. A., Seia, M., Piuma, C., Solbiati, M., Tobaldini, E., Ferrero, S., Montano, N., Costantino, G., & Buoli, M. (2022). Mental health and the effects on methylation of stress-related genes in front-line versus other health care professionals during the second wave of COVID-19 pandemic: an Italian pilot study. *European Archives of Psychiatry and Clinical Neuroscience, 273*(2), 347–356. https://doi.org/10.1007/s00406-022-01472-y

United Nations. (1993). Declaration on the Elimination of Violence against Women. In *UN Human Rights Office* (General Assembly resolution 48/104). Retrieved January 9, 2024, from https://www.ohchr.org/en/instruments-mechanisms/instruments/declaration elimination-violence-against-women

World Health Organization. (2013). Global and regional estimates of violence against women: prevalence and health effects of intimate partner violence and non-partner sexual violence. In *World Health Organization Publications* (ISBN: 978 92 4 156462 5). Retrieved January 9, 2024, from https://www.who.int/publications/i/item/9789241564625

World Health Organization. (2022). *ICD-11: International classification of diseases* (11th revision). https://icd.who.int/

Yehuda, R., Daskalakis, N. P., Lehrner, A., Désarnaud, F., Bader, H. N., Makotkine, I., Flory, J. D., Bierer, L. M., & Meaney, M. J. (2014). Influences of maternal and paternal PTSD on epigenetic regulation of the glucocorticoid receptor gene in Holocaust survivor offspring. *American Journal of Psychiatry, 171*(8), 872–880. https://doi.org/10.1176/appi.ajp.2014.13121571

Yu, X. W., Pandey, K., Katzman, A., & Alberini, C. M. (2020). A role for CIM6P/IGF2 receptor in memory consolidation and enhancement. *eLife, 9*. https://doi.org/10.7554/elife.54781

Zhang, L., Lu, Q., & Chang, C. (2020a). Epigenetics in health and disease. In *Advances in Experimental Medicine and Biology* (pp. 3–55). Springer.

Zhang, L., Pan, J., Chen, W., Jiang, J., & Huang, J. (2020b). Chronic stress-induced immune dysregulation in cancer: Implications for initiation, progression, metastasis, and treatment. *PubMed, 10*(5), 1294–1307. https://pubmed.ncbi.nlm.nih.gov/32509380

Barbara Segatto and Valentina Amerighi

Caring for those who are left behind: Social workers care for children affected by femicides

Abstract: The research focussed on the professionals who care for children orphaned as a result of femicide. Caring for these children means acting swiftly and deliberately, but it also means putting oneself in a position of great vulnerability, with exposure to criticism and error, the results of which could further harm the lives of the children involved and their network. Given the lack of specific training on the subject and the growing number of cases, we considered it essential to investigate how the social workers responsible for caring for children in vulnerable situations dealt with this specific case and what they feel they need to work in the children's best interests. Six social workers agreed to participate in the research and the be interviewed. All interviews were recorded and subsequently transcribed to then be analysed through a thematic content analysis. The interviewees' answers reveal the perspective and experiences of social workers who deal with minors orphaned as a result of femicide. The results underline the widespread deep trauma experienced by the social workers themselves and a lack of appropriate tools to reach effective goals.

Introduction

Femicide was recognized internationally a few decades ago, and since 2008 in Italy. However, Italian Law 4 of 11 January 2018, with *"amendments to the Civil Code, the Criminal Code, the Code of Criminal Procedure and other provisions in favour of orphans for domestic crimes"*, marked a first real turning point by recognizing the specific and profound complexities of this issue, which had previously been merged with others. The law establishes various interventions: from an economic viewpoint, the State is responsible for providing necessary support for the children (minors or dependent adults) of a parent killed by the other (Article 1), plus a series of precautions to prevent the offender from inheriting the deceased parent's estate and disposing of its assets (Articles 5 and 7). The same law also makes supports available to children who are orphaned by domestic crimes (Article 8) – with free medical and psychological care until full recovery – and allows them to change their surname (Article 13) (Torlone, 2019). The law, however, is not without its flaws. One of the greatest, perhaps, is the lack of any specific measures for foster families, despite the type of economic resources – and not only – that they require (Department of Family Policy, 2020). So, for now, Law 4/2018 cannot be considered complete. It is, however, a symbol, a first step that requires that we distance ourselves from a negationist and emergency-based attitude toward crimes of femicide and its collateral victims, so-called "special orphans" (Baldry, 2017).

Whenever social workers at any child protection service in Italy faces such a situation, they have no procedures to follow or guidelines to direct their action. Furthermore, little research is available on the subject and there has been no sharing of experience by those who have handled cases involving a woman who has been killed, a man who has committed violence, and one or more orphaned children.

To fill this gap in the protection process, an invitation to tender was launched in 2021, promoted by the *Con i Bambini* foundation as part of the fund to combat child educational poverty, allocating ten million euros to establish projects for orphans of domestic crimes and for foster families. (CISMAI, 2021) The tender called for research and action in various areas: from multi-dimensional and personalized care, to active research on the ground into "special orphans", to assessment of their physical and psychological well-being and analysis of their needs, as well as listening to foster families to meet their material and organizational needs (Zancaner, 2021).

At the time of planning the present research, the actions of this project funded by *Con i Bambini* had not yet started. Within the context outlined so far, we considered it useful to collect the viewpoints of social workers at regional child protection services who protect these special orphans and seek to appropriately respond to their needs. We sought to collect their experiences and information on what is already in place and what remains to be done to improve the assistance provided to these children.

At the time of planning the present research, the actions of this project funded by *Con i Bambini* had not yet started. Within the context outlined so far, we considered it useful to collect the viewpoints of social workers at regional child protection services who protect these special orphans and seek to appropriately respond to their needs. We sought to collect their experiences and information on what is already in place and what remains to be done to improve the assistance provided to these children.

The effects of femicide on children

Femicide is any act of violence based on gender discrimination causing the death of a woman, whether committed in public or private by any individual. The definition of the European Institute of Gender Equality (EIGE) (2017):

The killing of a woman by an intimate partner and the death of a woman as a result
of a practice that is harmful to women. Intimate partner is understood as a former or
current spouse or partner, whether or not the perpetrator shares or has shared the same
residence with the victim,

highlights the nature of the phenomenon as the dramatic outcome of a relationship with a violent intimate partner, whether the relationship has ended or is in
existence.

The survivors of femicide – often the children of these women – face a complex reality in order to continue their life without distressing deviances. To do
so, they require significant support and calibrated actions for their protection
(Baldry, 2017).

The murder of a mother hinders her child's psychological and emotional
development through exposure to a highly traumatic event, with social, relational, and family repercussions that impact their development (Carlson et al.,
2019). Femicide also deprives them of both parental figures, their certainties –
albeit controversial – and their notion of the "future" (Biginelli, 2020).

Unfortunately, the lack of research prevents us from identifying the actual
incidence and intensity of the physical and psychological disorders that children
may suffer as a result of their mother's murder. The few investigations conducted
to date have not involved large numbers of subjects and, generally, the people
who participated in the research had experienced the traumatic event a long time
before, making it difficult to trace the psychological outcomes clearly related to
the tragic experience specifically and with scientific accuracy (Alisic et al., 2015;
2017; Pitcho-Prelorentzos et al., 2021). Despite these limitations, however, existing research shows that children who witness the murder or who are present
at the time of the crime suffer more intense trauma (Ferrara et al., 2015), are
more easily subjected to victimization on several fronts (Miranda et al., 2021),
and have a higher probability of developing sleep disorders, fear of the dark and
of being left alone, recurrent destructive thoughts of the death of their mother,
and frequent emotional detachment (Hardesty et al., 2008). It is estimated that
many of the children suffering most from post-traumatic stress disorder (PTSD)
are female, although available data suggests that this results from a combination
of higher risk factors, such as greater exposure to sexual violence and a sense of
duty and care that is culturally conveyed and internalized in the female gender
(Akbaş & Karataş, 2020; Pitcho-Prelorentzos et al., 2021). Unfortunately, there
is insufficient data on the internal and external factors of protection and their
combination with risk factors and coping mechanisms (Hardesty et al., 2008).

In addition to the problems directly affecting these children and adolescents,
there are vulnerabilities associated with their placement following the loss of

their parents. The removal of minors from their family is the focus of significant debate in Italy, so it is striking that when it comes to serious cases, such as special orphans, there tends to be an excessive degree of simplification in the choices maintaining family relationships. While this satisfies the need for affective continuity and timeliness in the face of an event as tragic as femicide, it also releases social services from having to more carefully consider the most appropriate placement for the child. Maintaining relationships with parental networks is not necessarily strategically effective. For example, children are usually placed with the maternal grandparents, and in some cases, but more rarely, the paternal grandparents (the parents of the murderer), but subjecting a child who has already lost a parent to a high statistical probability of also losing their grandparents due to age is a risky choice. In addition, grandparents are often not sufficiently prepared to cope with such a complex parenting situation. It requires caring for minors who have experienced a highly traumatic event, which they may have witnessed, and who probably lived in a climate of violence that included repeated beatings over time of which they were aware. Additionally, because they are related to the victim, the grandparents could suffer guilt and be unable to accept what happened, unconsciously neglecting the task of care and development entrusted to them. Insufficient expression of mourning can have a devastating impact on a minor and can lead to withdrawal from social relations, school and life (Cassibba et al., 2012), aggravating all of the pathological conditions mentioned above. In addition, it is important to consider that living with grandparents may force the child to take a position with respect to the murder, with conflicting loyalties toward the mother, but also toward the father (Akbaş & Karataş, 2020; Corsello et al., 2018; Miranda et al., 2021). While these considerations do not rule out custody being assigned to grandparents, they do reveal established dynamics in child protection services and in juvenile courts, which do not always appear to be based on considerations focussing on the best interests of the child.

Whatever the choice of placement, research shows that assistance for caregivers from social services is decisive in achieving a balance between the child and the family (Hardesty et al., 2008). Indeed, the child may experience a conflict between their need to process what has happened and their fear of hurting, frightening or making the other person feel uncomfortable. Some foster parents may hesitate to address the situation to avoid upsetting the child or to protect themselves from powerful and highly emotional content that they feel ill equipped to handle (Weiss, 2014). Whatever their motivations, their reluctance to discuss the child's feelings damages the child's trust in adults: failure to meet their desire and need to be heard, disappointment in not being considered a credible source simply because they are a child undermines the already fragile foundations on which they build their relationship with the world of "grown-ups" (Callaghan et al., 2017).

Research with social workers

Objectives and method

The overall objective of this research is to investigate the perspectives and patterns of intervention adopted by social workers when working with children orphaned by femicide. The goal was to provide a space for the voices of social workers who are involved in building protection pathways for these children. By collecting the points of view of those who work closely with the challenges and unique nature of these cases, we wanted to obtain a more accurate picture of the phenomenon and the response provided by social services. To achieve this goal, we required a flexible tool that would allow us to explore the relevant topics in depth without precluding access to new information. We used the biographical interview (Bichi, 2002), a non-directive interview characterized by reframing by the interviewer, with no binding structure, and with the same situation-specific questions for everyone. The flexibility offered by this tool maked it possible to better explore the respondents' viewpoints through three main macro-themes: management of the specific case, the recasting of one's own experience, and acknowledged critical issues and obstacles.

We used the email addresses of child protection services in the Veneto region to identify social workers to interview. We drafted and sent an email presenting the research, requesting an interview with social workers having handled a case involving one or more children orphaned through femicide. We sent out 254 emails, receiving only 45 replies, of which 6 confirmed acceptance to participate in the research and to be interviewed.

Only one interview was held in person, with the remaining five conducted online. The shortest interview lasted forty-five minutes and the longest three and a half hours. All of the interviews were recorded and subsequently transcribed, then analysed based on a thematic analysis of the content (Riessman, 2008). Textual analysis was done manually, identifying three main themes: (1) loss of contact with the minors, (2) emotions related to handling femicide cases, and (3) professional critical issues in managing such cases.

The results

Despite our empirical reference set including only six professionals, the interviews revealed both a variety of positions and important shared views on the recurring themes.

The emotional point of view emerged involuntarily, as in the case of the **taboo of death**, or more thoughtfully as in the case of "**if I could do it over again**".

In almost all interviews (four of six), we were struck by the social workers' avoidance of the subject and their desire not to use words such as "murder, femicide, killed, death". This characterized many of the interviews, especially those with the social workers who still have very vivid memories of the case.

> *The kids had already been in foster care for some time. Even before the … the … […] when … it happened … (Interview 2)*
> *But it was the first time I'd ever worked with someone with this type of experience, so … […] I think that the episode …[…] the police called me in the morning saying, "Two hours ago there was this episode, there are children who need to be put into care." (Interview 3)*
> *The moment the incident occurred. Well, it was very unusual. (Interview 5)*

The attitude was different for the hypothesis of "**if I could do it over again**": there is a clear dividing line between the respondents who think that they could have done more and those who think that they did everything possible without this, however, being sufficient.

> *The question is: "Maybe I could have done something more to prevent it. Maybe I could have done something, I don't know…" (Interview 6)*
> *These are situations you never imagine, even though we were working with this person, who I assisted through the entire separation phase, but you never think someone could do something like that. And he had been stalking her, he'd stand outside the house, he kept pressuring her not to leave him. He kept calling her to get back together… maybe we weren't aware of the risk, the signs of the risk. (Interview 1)*
> *I remember my colleague saying to me: 'We did everything we could.' In the sense that for all the women we assist, we know something like this could happen. It only happened this time and she is the only woman we lost. (Interview 4)*

Another situation of symmetry is seen in the **loss of contact** with the orphaned children and, therefore, the consequent impossibility of knowing what had become of them and their individual path.

> *I don't know how things went after that and I don't know how the children grew up. […] I lost track of them. (Interview 1)*
> *I saw him when it came time to demand child support, so basically our involvement was limited to that. During these talks, the girl talked to me about the situation and we did a follow-up, but in fact, I don't remember doing anything specific. I really don't remember. I only remember child support. […] No… we don't know what happened after that, we don't know… (Interview 3)*
> *The mum wasn't from here… […] so the little girl moved to her mother's country of origin. And then, we sort of lost track of her. (Interview 4)*

There are numerous references to **obstacles to successful professional intervention** related to a lack of specific training, not so much on special orphans in particular, but more generally on the issue of child protection, and the need for social workers to not have to make decisions on such sensitive issues alone, because the lack of specific preparation and the complexity of the cases represent an externally critical mix.

> *I think, as a social worker, you have to make choices that will forever affect the life of that child, their parents, their siblings, later generations, and previous generations. This is an excessive burden for me because I don't think I have enough preparation and support. I started working in a child protection team when I had never worked in the field before, and no one ever told me there was special training.* (Interview 6)
>
> *What am I supposed to do?! Do I report a situation or not, knowing that by reporting it, I help the child, but at the same time I cause suffering to the family member? And most of all, personally, it creates a kind of conflict that puts me in a vulnerable, dangerous position.* (Interview 3)
>
> *Plus, and I think this is important, there's the question of always ensuring that there is a team working on the case. I'm thinking of my municipal colleagues who have full protection authority and who find themselves – even in very small municipalities – dealing with these sorts of situations. I think it's very difficult. It is essential to create multidisciplinary teams, including specialised services. Because as a municipality, you can address certain aspects of that situation, but then there are whole other series of aspects that require other skills, so you also have to network with specialised services.* (Interview 5)

They all touched on the issue of **family placement**, but were divided on the importance or otherwise of maintaining ties with the family of origin.

> *She was always placed with her grandmother, who is a relative within the fourth degree and in every respect, unless there are negative elements against her, her granddaughter can be entrusted to her. There was nothing… There was nothing that made us think that the grandmother was not dependable. […] I think the child should be removed only in extreme cases. They're still their dad, their mum, their siblings.* (Interview 6)
>
> *I've handled three cases: in two of them, the child was placed with the maternal family, and in the third with the paternal grandparents. The parents of this guy who's in prison said that the father was working in […]. but also the parents who lost their daughter, how can they get an appropriate defence?! Maintaining family ties is a decision that has to be taken carefully because they're certainly good people, but over time, even the behaviours with the other grandmother were no help.* (Interview 1)

Perhaps the topic that triggered the strongest emotions was **supervision**. All of the social workers expressed the need for greater use of this tool, to both protect and use their professionalism and skills through meeting with the *other*.

> *Right now, I find it a little difficult to understand what might be good for this child. That's why I ask for supervision. Because I need to take a different look and figure out what to do*

in this situation, what is the right thing to do. Because I don't know how good what we're doing is for this minor. [...] (Interview 5)

I asked for supervision [...]. I needed to work through what happened with someone else, and I also needed someone to tell me it wasn't my fault. No one asked how we were doing, how we were dealing with it, if we felt able to move on because it wasn't easy. [...] I was humanly sorry for that woman's death and for that little girl's lifelong wound. Not only as a professional, but as a person. (Interview 6)

Finally, we discussed the issue of guidelines and protection against subjective initiatives by social workers. Here, too, we found a significant degree of agreement.

Guidelines can certainly be helpful. I think it's important to ensure these children receive psychological support, whether they want it or not, because they have to face a load of pain but also some really heavy dynamics... (Interview 2)

These types of cases are so rare locally that it would be useful to have national guidelines. Placement, for example, you don't have much time to decide what to do... If the woman was killed that day, you have to place the child by the evening... You have less than twenty-four hours...There's nothing to tell you what elements you can evaluate quickly. (Interview 3)

I don't know, when it happened, I expected someone would help us... someone would help us figure out... what to do. Even though I had worked at child protection services for thirteen years, I felt really helpless. I didn't know what to do and I remember really needing to talk to someone about it, but... nobody listened. (Interview 6)

Discussion

Our respondents' statements allowed us to identify a critical framework with regard to the care of special orphans in our country that still seems unable to guarantee adequate protection of the rights and well-being of these children and adolescents.

We see that there are no specific tools available to social workers: no guidelines, no recommendations or best practices. This absence forces individual social workers to come up with an ad hoc solution on their own frequently without even being able to count on the support of a team or a supervisor. The choice of placement, as well as the way in which family members meet the child, the number and type of interviews, the relationship with school and the community cannot be based only on a single social worker's subjective considerations but require common operational strategic guidelines to provide guidance and facilitate the time of care and decision making.

Furthermore, in our country, each child protection service is dependent on different organizations: there may be a single team or intra-professional teams, there may be different levels of attention to the economic factor than to support and assistance, there may be different resources available to social workers. Because of all these aspects, the interventions carried out are subject to such wide variability and discretion that they cannot guarantee fairness in the response offered (Segatto et al., 2020).

Again, in our country, the children orphaned by femicide, and the families who take them in are often not monitored for a sufficiently long time to receive the support and therapies they need to cope with their traumatic loss, despite this type of lack potentially having very serious repercussions on the child's physical and psychological health. In fact, most of the social workers we interviewed said that they had lost contact with the orphaned minors after the femicide, demonstrating that after initial interventions, no further specific attention was offered to them by the institutions responsible for child protection. Instead, everything is left up to the individual family.

Finally, it is important to emphasize that participation in this project was slight, due not only to the small number of cases but also to the social workers' unwillingness to talk about them. Five of the professionals we contacted refused to discuss them. The reasons they gave were not so much about protecting privacy or the fear that this data would be used inappropriately, as the belief that there wasn't much to say, that they did not have great tools at their disposal and that they were unwilling to relive such traumatic events. This last reason harkens back to a possible vicarious or secondary trauma (McCann & Pearlman, 1990) that social workers who handle these specific cases may suffer. They would have to assume the traumatic experience of the users at an emotional level such as to experience perceptions of themselves that are incapacitating with respect to their self-effectiveness and their therapeutic power (Lundberg & Bergmark, 2018; Witt & Diaz, 2018) and that therefore interfere in their work if not addressed and processed through appropriate therapy.

For the future, it appears important to be able to establish specialist teams at the regional level for children orphaned through femicide. These teams should include professionals trained in the issue and whose work is based on best practices and protocols. Until this becomes reality, it would be advisable to provide the social workers who care for these special orphans both supervision and emotional support to process possible secondary trauma.

References

Akbaş, G. E., & Karataş, K. (2020). The depth of trauma: The children left behind after femicide in Turkey. *International Social Work, 0*.

Alisic, E., Krishna, R. N., Groot, A., & Frederick J., W. (2015). Children's mental health and well-being after parental intimate partner homicide: A systematic review. *Clinical Child and Family Psychology Review, 18*, 328.

Alisic, E., Groot, A., Snetselaar, H., Stroeken, T., & de Putte E., V. (2017). Children bereaved by fatal intimate partner violence: A population-based study into demographics, family characteristics and homicide exposure. *Plos One, 12*, e0183466.

Baldry, A. C. (2017). *Orfani speciali: Chi sono, dove sono, con chi sono. Conseguenze psico-sociali su figlie e figli del femminicidio*. Milan, FrancoAngeli.

Bichi, R. (2002). *L'intervista biografica. Una proposta metodologica*. Milan, Vita e Pensiero.

Biginelli, C. (2020),. Danni da femminicidio: quale tutela per gli orfani? in "MINORIGIUSTIZIA" 3/2020, pp 199-205, DOI: 10.3280/MG2020-003022

Callaghan, J. E. M., Fellin, L. C., Mavrou, S., Alexander, J., & Sixsmith, J. (2017). The management of disclosure in children's accounts of domestic violence: Practices of telling and not telling. *Journal of Child and Family Studies, 26*(12), 3370–3387.

Carlson, J., Voith, L., Brown, J. C., & Holmes, M. (2019). Viewing children's exposure to intimate partner violence through a developmental, social-ecological, and survivor lens: The current state of the field, challenges, and future directions. *Violence Against Women, 25*, 6–28.

Cassibba, R., Elia, L., & Terlizzi, M. (2012). L'accompagnamento del bambino e delle famiglie (biologica e affidataria) nel percorso dell'affidamento familiare. *Minori&Giustizia, 1*, 269–277.

CISMAI & Terre Des Hommes. (2021). *Seconda Indagine Nazionale sul maltrattamento di bambini e adolescenti in Italia*. Autorità Garante dell'Infanzia e Adolescenza. Available at: https://www.garanteinfanzia.org/sites/default/files/2021-07/ii-indagine-nazionale-maltrattamento-2021.pdf

Corsello, G., Ianniello, F., Semeraro, L., Franceschini, G., Scalzo, L. L., Giardino, I., & Ferrara, P. (2018). Murdered women's children: A social emergency and gloomy reality. *Signa Vitae, 14*, 71–74.

Dipartimento per le politiche della famiglia. (2020). *Report di Analisi dei dati secondari e primari di livello nazionale e regionale 2019/2020*. Available at: http://www.poninclusionefamiglia.it/wp-content/uploads/2019/05/REPORT-ANALISI-DATI-NAZIONALI-2020-PER-PUBBLICAZIONE.pdf.

Ferrara, P., Caporale, O., Cutrona, C., Sbordone, A., Amato, M., Spina, G., & Scambia, G. (2015). Femicide and murdered women's children: Which future for these children orphans of a living parent? *Italian Journal of Pediatrics, 41*.

Hardesty, J. L., Campbell, J. C., McFarlane, J. M., & Lewandowski, L. A. (2008). How children and their caregivers adjust after intimate partner femicide. *Journal of Family Issues*, 29(1), 100–124.

Lundberg, L., & Bergmark, Å. (2018). Self-perceived competence and willingness to ask about intimate partner violence among Swedish social workers. *European Journal of Social Work*, 24, 1–12.

McCann, I. L., & Pearlman, L. A. (1990). Vicarious traumatization: A framework for understanding the psychological effects of working with victims. *Journal of Traumatic Stress*, 3(1), 131–149.

Miranda, J., Crockett, M., & Vera Pavez, J. (2021). The co-occurrence of intimate partner violence exposure with other victimizations: A nationally representative survey of Chilean adolescents. *Child Abuse & Neglect, 117.*

Pitcho-Prelorentzos, S., Leshem, E., & Mahat-Shamir, M. (2021). Shattered Voices: Daughters' Meaning Reconstruction in Loss of a Mother to Intimate Partner Homicide. *Journal of Interpersonal Violence.*

Riessman, C. K. (2008). *Narrative methods for the human sciences.* CA, USA: Sage.

Segatto, B., Dal Ben, A., & Giacomin, S. (2020): The use of discretion in decision-making by social workers at child protection services in Italy. *European Journal of Social Work.*

Torlone, G. (2019). *Femminicidi, Una Legge per gli Orfani Speciali.* Available at: https://www.lumsanews.it/figli-vittima-un-assassino-legge-gli-orfani-speciali/

Weiss, N. (2014). *Research under duress: Resonance and distance in ethnographic fieldwork.* In I. Maček (Ed.), *Engaging violence. Trauma, memory and representation* (pp. 127–139). London: Routledge.

Witt L., Diaz C. (2018). Social workers' attitudes towards female victims of domestic violence: A study in one English local authority. Child and Family social work, https://doi.org/10.1111/cfs.12604

Zancaner, L. (2021). *Femminicidi, Parte in Italia il primo progetto per gli orfani.* Available at: https://alleyoop.ilsole24ore.com/2021/07/28/femminicidi-orfani/?refresh_ce=1.

Assunta Penna and Debora Maria Pizzimenti

The internalized violence within online platforms

Abstract: In pervasive digital environments, hate speech manifests its distinct exhibition and reach: sexist comments and threats, racist insults, and homophobic attacks find an ideal space to express themselves online. Generally, women predominantly become targets of online hate speech. Within these spaces, our study aims to contemplate the dynamics contributing to the internalization of misogyny and the adoption of self-deprecating attitudes among women identified as *Femcels*. Employing *digital media ethnography*, we examined the Femcel discussion platform known as "Crystalcafe", exploring how patriarchy, internalized misogyny, and lookism interact and shape the experiences of its users. This preliminary analysis reveals the emergence of unrealistic expectations regarding beauty and personal fulfillment through successful romantic relationships. These expectations push women into self-blame for their involuntary single status.

Introduction to the topic

The digital revolution, termed as a "contemporary mythology" (Balbi, 2022), denotes the social changes resulting from the widespread and continuous use of digital technologies, bringing forth a series of significant and intricate transformations within social interactions, societal structures, and everyday life. The opportunities presented by digital interconnection, driven by "liquid modernity", can yield critical implications on the "fragilization" of human relationships (Bauman, 2014), fostering sentiments of loneliness, alienation, and emotional isolation coming from hyperconnectivity when genuine human connection fails, *alone together* (Turkle, 2019). Giddens (1995) has previously examined the transformations occurring within the private sphere of gender relations, sexuality, and love. Drawing upon sociological, historical, and literary sources, his analysis emphasizes various aspects that led to the sexual revolution, elucidating its deeper significance beyond sentimental grounds. The sexual revolution of the 1960s significantly depersonalized relationships that presupposed stability (Carzo et al., 2007). It is shown in a transformation of intimacy, leading to rapid, superficial, occasional encounters devoid of a life plan solely linked to marriage. This restructuring of the intimate sphere, according to the author, will lead to the democratization of the private sphere and the affirmation of personal autonomy (Giddens, 1995).

In the platformized society (van Dijck et al., 2018), the pervasive and intrusive nature of technologies – evident in their ability to infiltrate individuals' digital personal spaces – accelerates the desiccation of relationships, enhancing the pervasiveness of gender-based violence. An aspect to consider in this context is the global reach of online violence against women and the speed at which content can disseminate across the net. The rapid and widespread dissemination further amplifies the negative impact of these forms of violence. This expansive complexity, not confined by geographical boundaries and often eluding traditional control and regulatory rules.

The diffusion and accessibility of anonymous online platforms (van Dijk et al. 2018) have provided fertile ground for open and often explicit discussions on a wide range of topics, including those related to mental health and psychophysical well-being. Particularly within the Femcel community (Kay, 2022), the anonymity and freedom of expression offered by these spaces have led to the openness and sharing of personal experiences but have also raised questions about the potential negative implications coming from these interactions. These digital spaces, with their open and often unrestrictive nature, can significantly impact the well-being of individuals involved. While on one hand, these anonymous platforms can offer a supportive environment and mutual understanding, on the other, they may foster the identification and normalization of dysfunctional or pathological behaviors (Illouz, 2019), as well as chain reactions that can fuel a cycle where negative or dysfunctional experiences are amplified through a sort of feedback loop within echo chambers (Sunstein, 2017; Boccia Artieri & Farci, 2020), exacerbating the issue rather than providing solutions or support. Additionally, these environments can reinforce self-destructive or distorted beliefs regarding one's self-image, self-esteem, and ability to cope with daily challenges.

In this intricate scenario, our work aims to investigate the dynamics contributing to the internalization of misogynistic violence and the adoption of self-depreciating attitudes among women identifying as Femcels. Femcels are women who identify with the Incel subculture and share the experience of being unable to find a romantic or sexual relationship, despite the desire for a partner. They keenly feel excluded from the sexual market, where "high-quality"[1]

---

1   These are women who exhibit physical traits aligned with traditional beauty standards, such as a captivating appearance, a slender figure, symmetrical facial features, smooth and glossy hair, and other attributes commonly regarded as attractive according to prevailing beauty norms.

women monopolize male attention, leaving less attractive women deprived of it (Kay, 2022, p. 36). The objective of this research is to explore whether and how these women adhere to or react to misogyny and patriarchal standards, aiming to deepen the understanding of the factors shaping their individual experiences and the role of their digital life in shaping their identification (Delli Paoli & Masullo, 2022). Specifically, we focus on the notion that the *male gaze* (Mulvey, 1975), which judges women, seems to have also influenced women themselves, leading them to constantly judge themselves as inadequate (Capecchi, 2022). In a previous study, whose methodology we also apply in the present work, we conducted an in-depth analysis of the feelings of anger and exclusion experienced by women who identify as femcels and gather on the Vindicta platform (Pizzimenti, Penna 2024). This platform is part of the broader Femcelosphere, which is conceptualized as an umbrella term encompassing different identities and a wide range of attitudes, united by frustration, suffering, and humiliation resulting from involuntary singlehood. This analysis contributes to a broader reflection on internalized misogyny and the ways in which women respond to and resist patriarchal logics. Its highlighting the complex interplay between personal identity, social dynamics, and structures of oppression. A violence, "less recognizable because invisible, powerful because ancient: a form of dominance inscribed in the social order, operating in the obscurity of bodies and souls through the imagination, feelings, emotions, and habits of men and women" (Priulla, 2023, p. 87). According to our analysis, this phenomenon acts in an internalized form even within online communities that actively claim to combat stereotypes and offensive models. The conceptualization of beauty is linked to the process that defines a user's value in terms dependent on the observer and their approval.

"As a consequence, dependence on others (and not only men) tends to become constitutive of their being [...] Continuously under the gaze of others, women are condemned constantly to experience the discrepancy between the real body to which they are bound and the ideal body towards which they endlessly strive" (Bourdieu, 1998, pp. 66–68). The sexually objectified individual finds themselves, in fact, in an inferior position compared to those who wield the power to define their value (Illouz, 2019, pp. 149–150).

A significant aspect related to this dynamic is that sexualization fosters a belief that attractive physical appearance is crucial not only for attracting the opposite sex but also for achieving success in all areas of life. This belief, in turn, fuels the process of "self-objectification", where there is a tendency to internalize the sexual gaze, emphasizing outward appearance as a central element of one's self-esteem and self-evaluation (Calogero et al., 2011, pp. 53–54). In a contemporary perspective, Sheila Jeffreys' work (2015) describes internalized misogyny as the phenomenon in which women absorb and adopt misogynistic attitudes, beliefs, and behaviors as part of their own identity. Jeffreys indicates that the fashion and beauty industry has taken a predominant role in defining and regulating femininity, pushing women to conform to unrealistic beauty ideals that often require invasive and harmful interventions. These practices, coupled with the internalization of values promoting sexu,al objectification, contribute to women's subordination in the social and cultural context. This internalization may lead women to judge themselves and other women according to patriarchal standards and expectations, adopting behaviors and attitudes that perpetuate their own state of subordination. These practices not only harm women's physical and mental health but also limit their opportunities to achieve full and equal human status (MacKinnon, 2006). According to Naomi Wolf, "The qualities that a given period calls beautiful in women are merely symbols of the female behavior that that period considers desirable: *The beauty myth is always actually prescribing behavior and not appearance*" (Wolf, 2022, p. 14). In this perspective, internalized misogyny can manifest in various ways, including constant self-criticism, rivalry among women, dependence on patriarchy for one's sense of worth, and the devaluation of female experiences. Internalized misogyny is a result of socialization and assimilation of patriarchal values and norms affecting women themselves.

The insidious shadow of misogyny in the beauty cult: Current practices

In recent years, the proliferation of online harassment has surged, in line with the increased use of social networks. The spread of misogynistic discourse and discrimination on social media and forums has raised concerns about its social consequences. Facebook, with over 35 million users in Italy and nearly three billion worldwide, highlights negative impacts, such as 40 % of girls under 25 experiencing threats or harassment. Women from ethnic and sexual minorities appear particularly vulnerable, facing gender, ethnic, and sexual orientation-based abuses. Instagram and WhatsApp, both owned by Meta (formerly Facebook), encounter similar issues, with widespread non-consensual pornography fuelling online violence and women's distrust (Giugni, 2022). At the same time, sites like 4chan and other platforms belonging to the "manosphere" mainly host a male audience (Statista.com 2019), providing fertile ground for misogynistic discussions perpetuated by "red-pilled" and Incel (involuntary celibate) individuals (Dolce & Pilla, 2019; Nagle, 2018; Ging, 2017; Pizzimenti & Pasciuto, 2022). According to recent research (Amnesty International, 2018; Knight, 2019; The Economist, 2021; Wolf, 2022), more than a third of women have experienced online aggression, negatively impacting mental health and physical safety. Virtual violence affects the victims' "real" lives (EIGE, 2017). While the harmful impacts of online misogyny are largely decoded, an equally significant yet less explored area concerns the response of Femcel women. In the realm of "Femcel" communities (Kay, 2022; Ling, 2022), the influence of the *male gaze* emerges as a powerful force shaping women's self-perceptions. The term Femcel is an adaptation of Incel and refers to women who consider themselves excluded or marginalized from cultures of intimacy and sex (Kay, 2022, p. 29) due to their physical appearance or other mental health-related issues. Constant evaluation based on society's beauty ideals affects users' self-esteem, often leading them to internalize and adopt these ideals as a criterion for self-assessment. As Incels, Femcels also utilize forums and online discussion platforms to share their experiences of loneliness, rejection, and humiliation (Kay, 2022; Balci et al., 2023). In an era where the cult of beauty dominates global aesthetic standards, an insidious shadow emerges, infiltrating practices related to the concept of female beauty. Recent investigations reveal that, even among Western women considered secure, attractive, and successful, there lies a complex web of dark emotions (Wolf, 2022). In our analysis, it is clear how the phenomenon of "lookism" expresses "the sexual self, the technological self, and the consumer self are aligned in a single powerful matrix, relatively dissociated from the emotional self. The selfhood at the center of these processes is at once objectified and objectifying" (Illouz, 2019, p. 173). Within Femcel communities, a complex dynamic emerges where, on one hand, there is a strong inclination to react to beauty standards imposed by society, while, on the other hand, there is an accentuation of the importance given to adhering to prevailing ideals within these spaces. This duality reflects the socio-cultural pressures forcing women to conform to unrealistic models. The internalization of misogyny among Femcel women can be interpreted as the result of a complex process of socialization and cultural assimilation, where prevalent beauty and relational success standards in society have deeply rooted themselves in individual perceptions and attitudes. The persistence of unrealistic aesthetic ideals, often promoted and amplified by media and popular culture, has led many women to uncritically embrace these norms, generating a sense of inadequacy and insecurity regarding their own image and worth. Furthermore, the digital context has amplified women's exposure to messages and social representations emphasizing the centrality of physical appearance and relational gratification as fundamental criteria for self-realization. Simultaneously, Femcels engage in and exchange beauty advice to groom their appearance according to standards imposed by the male perspective, thus self-objectifying their bodies and transforming them into instruments to attract male attention. From this standpoint,

Femcel women find themselves trapped in a paradoxical situation, perceiving themselves as doubly marginalized by society. On one side, they lament their alleged lack of attractiveness and feel ostracized due to this presumed "ugliness", enduring external negative judgment that blames and marginalizes them. On the other hand, they grapple with the challenge of adhering to distorted and unattainable beauty ideals, leading to a sense of inadequacy and failure in attracting a romantic partner. This duality highlights a complex internal struggle where Femcel women contend with extremely restrictive beauty ideals that contribute to intensifying the persistent sense of inadequacy and social exclusion.

Research methodology

Based on the theoretical premises described above, the aim of this study is to understand the social and cultural dynamics within a specific digital context according to the perception of female ugliness/beauty and the internalization processes of misogyny, as well as the reactions and adaptations of Femcel women within the patriarchal system. The research questions undertaken are: How do adherence or resistance dynamics manifest themselves to the dominant beauty standards within Femcel online communities, and how do such responses reflect processes of adaptation or contestation of socially imposed aesthetic norms? Furthermore, how does the internalization of misogynistic models within female spaces, if it existed, contribute to the formation of attitudes and behaviors that conform to discriminatory cultural ideals towards women?

The methodology employed for observation is digital ethnography (Sumiala & Tikka, 2020), a qualitative research approach that adapts ethnographic techniques to the study of online social discussion spaces (Delli Paoli, 2021; Delli Paoli & D'Auria, 2021; Delli Paoli & Masullo, 2022). The chosen digital field is the Crystalcafe website, an international online imageboard. The selection of this digital space was motivated by its platform characteristics, specifically the uniqueness of its content (comments and threads), and its reputation for being frequented by individuals identifying as "Femcel". The observation period spanned from April to September 2023. Additionally, the choice of platform was driven by the need for a comprehensive understanding of the experiences lived by Femcel women within the digital community, with particular attention to the cultural and social aspects shaping self-perceptions and the dynamics of lookism (prejudice based on physical appearance) shared by users. The adopted methodology encompasses the classification of comments gathered from the Crystalcafe imageboard and a qualitative analysis aimed at capturing nuances and emerging themes from user testimonials. The selected comments collected on Crystalcafe are publicly available and accessible to anyone accessing the platform. The investigation was carried out through non-participant observation (Delli Paoli & Masullo, 2022) of the forum, allowing an external examination of the study environment to avoid any influence resulting from the observer's presence during the digital data collection process. This methodology has resulted particularly relevant considering the distinctive nature of the community and the anonymity of the study environment. The manually selected comments were subsequently categorized using NVivo software for digital material management (Coppola, 2011). Before being classified using NVivo software, user comments underwent an initial examination by the researcher. Subsequently, these comments were selected and stored in online PDF format. NVivo software facilitated the exploration of connections between different categories and subcategories, allowing for a broader and more detailed understanding of the social and cultural dynamics emerging from user discussions. The selection of comments and messages from the threads under investigation was conducted through a targeted approach (Patton, 1990; Delli Paoli & Masullo, 2022). Specifically, comments that elicited a significant level of user engagement, i.e. those that sparked a considerable number of interactions and responses, were collected and preserved. For the purposes of this analysis, a sample consisting of 909 comments was created, which underwent an in-depth process of qualitative content analysis. During the analysis, a deductive coding methodology was adopted to systematically categorize the comments under study into 8 subcategories and aggregate them into 3 main macro-categories developed considering the theoretical perspectives of Wolf (2022) and Jeffreys (2015) regarding the impacts of misogyny and its social influences on women. This categorization approach proved to be a valuable analytical tool for delineating the experiences shared by users, focussing on the perception of female ugliness (Kay, 2022), the processes of misogyny internalization, and the mechanisms of reaction or adherence to the patriarchal system (Wolf, 2022; Jeffreys, 2015). The division of comments into macro-categories and subcategories was defined as follows:

Table 1: Research categories.

Internalized misogyny
1   Underestimation of Women: Comments that belittle women's abilities or depict them as inferior to men.
2   Victim-Blaming: Comments that blame women for the violence they experience or downplay the impact of violence on their lives.
3   Perpetuation of Gender Stereotypes: Comments that reinforce traditional gender roles and harmful stereotypes regarding female behavior and appearance.

(continued)

Table 1:   Continued

Internalized misogyny

4	Adherence to Patriarchal Models: Comments that endorse and promote patriarchal values and discriminatory power hierarchies between men and women.

Reactions to Patriarchy and Negative Stereotypes

1	Empowerment Feminism: Comments that advocate for female autonomy, gender equality, and women's ability to choose their own path in society.
2	Critique of Male Chauvinism and Gender Discrimination: Comments that denounce gender inequalities, structural injustices, and discriminations faced by women due to patriarchy.
3	Promotion of Diversity and Inclusion: Comments that support the diversity of female experiences and identities, including those of women of colour, LGBTQ+ women, and other gender minorities.
4	Demand for Accountability: Comments that demand accountability and awareness regarding behaviors and actions perpetuating sexism and patriarchy.

Irrelevant Comments

-	Messages or observations that do not contribute to this research or are not related to the subject matter at hand.

Research findings and comments analysis

The research revealed that Crystalcafe is a space where women gather to discuss various topics related to femininity, beauty, and their personal experiences. On this platform, users share their thoughts and issues, providing mutual support in an environment that frequently involves detailed discussions on external pressures concerning beauty and physical attractiveness. Graphic 1 illustrates the distribution of selected comments within the Crystalcafe imageboard.

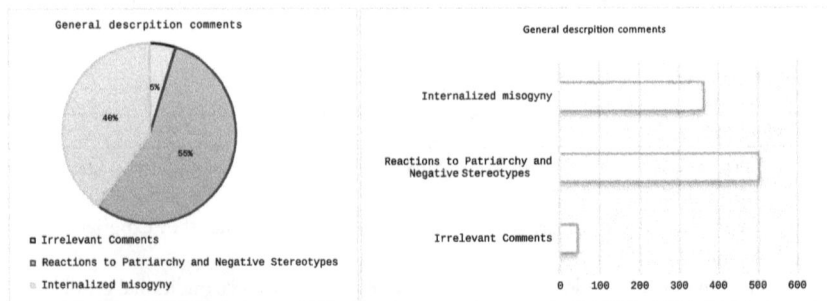

Figure 1: General comments (909)

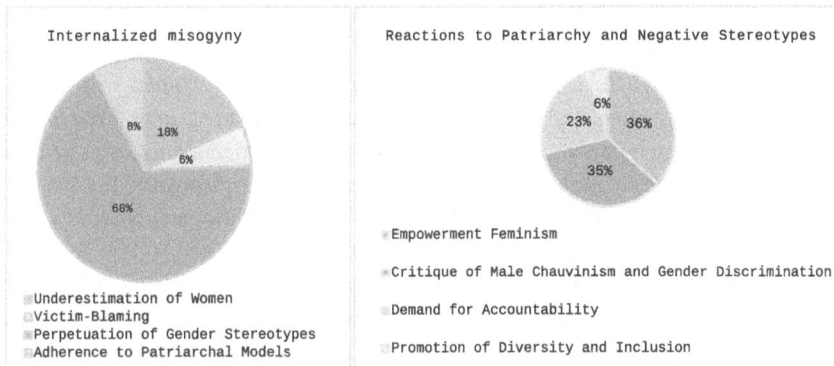

Figure 2: Internalized misogyny and Reactions to Patriarchy and Negative Stereotypes

The comments analysis revealed how the concept of beauty is often dictated by predetermined social standards, placing particular emphasis on physical features such as breast size:

Comments	
User 1	The main point of this thread and the other one is that medium-sized breasts are almost on the same level as large breasts. The small ones are still considered ugly by men.
User 2	Why do small breast threads always turn into a competition and hating women with larger breasts?
User 3	It happened with the big breast thread too, where someone said a woman needed a reduction
User 4	everyone says bigger breasts = more popular
User 5	Having small boobs has shattered my confidence, but also many other things. I'm a B cup and many men will tell me they're small.
User 6	I'm thinking of taking breast enlargement pills or estrogen. I hope it doesn't harm me

From the presented comments, here emerges the presence of groups exhibiting a hostile stance toward women with less prominent physical attributes, employing labels such as "flattie" and "Becky". The term "Becky" originates from the Incel (involuntary celibates) community and is used to refer to a woman considered as the ideal or average female partner for men. Becky represents a woman who might be perceived as attractive but not exceptionally beautiful or popular like Stacy, another term used in the Incel community. Within the Femcel subculture, Becky might embody a sort of average standard of female beauty that women may view as ideal or desirable, albeit not exceptional or particularly striking (Dolce & Pilla, 2019). It's intriguing to note how women with different breast sizes often find themselves in conflict, comparing male preferences regarding which type is deemed more attractive. For women identified as Femcel and active on the Crystalcafe platform, the concept of "large breasts" holds a significance like the attribute of "height" among Incels. Additionally, there is a tendency to openly criticize users declaring themselves to have considerable breast size, even without presenting other characteristics such as being "obese" or "unattractive". It's pertinent to underscore that this comparison among women frequently devolves into conflicts and rivalries, exhibiting attitudes similar to those observed among Incels, harbouring feelings of envy and aspiring to be like the presumed "Chad".

Comments	
User 7	Why has this (big breast) thread received fewer responses than the other?
User 8	1 If you have large breasts, the likelihood that you need support from the imageboard is lower because you tend to be more desired and have higher self-esteem.
	2 Since larger breasts are more desired, the perception of "big" and "small" is overall controversial. Above average isn't optimal by social standards, and consequently, most women with medium-sized breasts tend to think they have small breasts. It's like male height: 5'10" is above the average for American men, but for many, it's still considered "short."
	3 For some reason, users with larger breasts have decided not to post or haven't seen this thread because threads about small breasts always turn into a competition and breed hatred toward women with larger breasts.

In the same way, Femcel women, who perceive a lack of beauty and a sense of marginalization within society, develop a significant obsession with idealized female figures, often referred to as "Stacy" and the previously mentioned "Becky". It is observable that these women's self-esteem largely depends on the amount of attention they receive from men and the perception of their physical attractiveness. A critical stance toward patriarchal structures and negative gender stereotypes emerges from the comments, indicating that some Femcel individuals adopt a perspective actively challenging gender inequalities and discriminatory social norms. This response might signify active engagement within online or offline communities that promote female empowerment and feminism, coupled with a systematic critique of cultural conventions contributing to gender discrimination. However, it is crucial to note that individual reactions may change considerably, and not all members of the Femcel subculture necessarily adhere to such viewpoints or engage in forms of activism or political resistance.

Conclusion

Within the landscape of Femcel communities, the research work proposed highlights the presence of internalized misogyny as a phenomenon. Overall, during the observation of the platform, a substantial percentage of comments emerged related to both the macro-category of "Reactions to patriarchy and negative stereotypes" (55 %) and the macro-category of "Internalized misogyny" (40 %). Within this apparent polarization, likely attributable to the diverse ideologies of Femcel users, the presence of numerous comments in the category of "Perpetuation of gender stereotypes" (246 comments, 68 % of the Internalized misogyny macro-category) is significant. Beyond the percentage-based representation, particularly interesting, considering the research inquiries, was the analysis of comments where language permeated with sexism and misogyny fuels a polarized and divisive online environment. The most used terms include: "Pick-me girl" (referring to a woman willing to do anything to entice a man), "tradwife" (traditional wife), and "e-girl" (a girl who flirts with many guys when online). Femcels, perceiving themselves as excluded from social standards of beauty and acceptance, may internalize the idea that their lack of relational or social success stems from personal or physical flaws, adopting a highly self-deprecating and self-destructive perspective. This phenomenon can be considered a reflection of the social and cultural pressure imposing unattainable beauty standards on women, often inaccessible to the majority. The discourse on internalized misogyny within Femcel spaces can be observed in how women internalize and perpetuate patriarchal ideals that marginalize, subordinate, and discriminate against them. This internalization can lead women to evaluate themselves and other women based on aesthetically rigid criteria imposed by society, thus reinforcing gender oppression and contributing to the perpetuation of harmful stereotypes.

It has emerged that, despite the potential for creating a support network, such platforms can also perpetuate a culture that normalizes and amplifies unhealthy behaviors. The open sharing of negative experiences can have a contagious impact, influencing other members of the community and pushing them to identify with it or adopt dysfunctional attitudes (Turkle, 2019). Furthermore, the lack of regulation and the anonymous nature help the dissemination of non-professional advice, potentially harmful for those seeking support and guidance (boyd & Marwick, 2011; boyd, 2014). The harmful competition for body control that arises in these digital environments can contribute to worsening pre-existing conditions. The constant exposure to discussions related to physical appearance and prevailing aesthetic norms amplifies anxiety and concerns regarding the body, further exacerbating users' psychological challenges.

Considering Jeffreys' analysis on beauty as a tool of oppression and the merchandising of female beauty, the Femcel language and themes emerging from the analysis of these comments highlight the complexity of gender dynamics and the necessity for heightened critical awareness and social action aimed at deconstructing harmful patriarchal ideals. Despite the apparent commitment of the community to articulate discussions regarding female empowerment (see Figure 2) and mutual support among women, dynamics of individualism and competition emerge inhibiting the creation of authentic and lasting social cohesion. It is crucial to develop greater awareness regarding the spread and use of misogynistic or discriminatory attitudes, both online and in real life. Within online subcultures, often marginal and underground, traces of such forms of violence can be identified, sometimes unnoticed, sometimes acknowledged, or even tolerated without being confronted, thus fuelling their silent development. These implications call for a conscious and targeted response from institutions and communities to ensure a safe and inclusive digital environment for all individuals. Simultaneously, the analysis reveals how the phenomenon of "lookism" is closely intertwined with concepts of sexual, technological, and consumption individuality (Illouz, 2019). This complex and often distorted intersection plays a significant role in the objectification of individuals and the promotion of unrealistic aesthetic ideals.

The research is limited in its focus on textual content within the platform, overlooking the analysis of broader contexts such as the impact of images or the frequency and duration of online interactions. This research should be replicated in other communities for comparison and in the same community in the long run.

These factors could play a significant role in shaping the perceptions and experiences of Crystalcafe users. It would be pertinent to delve deeper, in future empirical investigations, into the relational dynamics and psychosocial implications of these digital spaces.

References

Amnesty International. (2018). *Troll Patrol Findings*.

Balbi, G. (2022). *L'ultima ideologia: breve storia della rivoluzione digitale*. Gius. Laterza.

Bauman, Z. (2014). *La vita tra reale e virtuale*. EGEA.

Balci, U., Ling, C., De Cristofaro, E., Squire, M., Stringhini, G., & Blackburn, J. (2023). *Beyond Fish and Bicycles: Exploring the Varieties of Online Women's*

Ideological Spaces. Published in the Proceedings of the 15th ACM Web Science Conference 2023 (ACM WebSci 2023).

Boccia Artieri, G., & Farci, M. (2020). Le emozioni dell'alt-right. La dimensione neoliberale e affettiva delle piattaforme. *Sociologia della comunicazione, 59,* pp. 83–107. DOI: 10.3280/SC2020-059005.

Bourdieu, P. (1998). *La domination masculine*. Ed. du Seuil (trad. en. 2001, *Masculine Domination*, Stanford University Press).

boyd, d., & Marwick, A. (2011). *Social Privacy in Networked Publics: Teen's Attitudes, Practices and Strategies*. Indirizzo internet: http://www.danah.org/papers/2011/SocialPrivacyPLSC-Draft.pdf [Accesso 20.12.2021].

boyd, d. (2014). *It's complicated: The social lives of networked teens*. Yale: Yale University Press.

Calogero, R. M., Tantleff-Dunn, S. E., & Thompson, J. (2011). *Self-objectification in women: Causes, consequences, and counteractions*. American Psychological Association, p. 53.

Capecchi, S. (2022). Media digitali, genere e sessualità. In M. Farci & C. Scarcelli (Eds.), *Media digitali, genere e sessualità*. Mondadori.

Carzo D., Cava A., & Salvo M., (2007). *Globalità virtuale e realtà locale. Genere, consumi e comunicazione in una città di provincia*. Franco Angeli.

Coppola, L. (2011). NVivo: un programma per l'analisi qualitativa, Franco Angeli, Milano.

Dolce, R., & Pilla, F. (2019). *Il web che odia le donne*. Ledizioni. Milano.

Jeffreys, S. (2015). *Beauty and Misogyny. Harmful cultural practices in the West* (2nd ed.). London: Routledge.

EIGE. (2017). *Violenza virtuale contro le donne e le ragazze*. https://eige.europa.eu/sites/default/files/documents/ti_pubpdf_mh0417543itn_pdfweb_20171026164002.pdf

Giddens, A. (1995). *La trasformazione dell'intimità*, trad. it.. Il Mulino.

Ging, D. (2017). Alphas, Betas, and Incels: Theorizing the masculinities of the Manosphere. *Men and Masculinities, 22*(4), 638–657.

Giugni, L. (2022). *La rete non ci salverà: Perché la rivoluzione digitale è sessista (e come resistere)*. Longanesi. http://www.voxdiritti.it/mappa-dellintolleranza-7-misoginia/

Illouz, E. (2019). *The end of love: A sociology of negative relations*. Oxford University Press.

Delli Paoli, A. (2021). Ethnography from physical to digital contexts: Principles and practices. In G. Punziano & A. Delli Paoli (Eds.), *Handbook of research on advanced research methodologies for a digital society* (pp. 196–216). Hershey, PA, USA: IGI Global.

Delli Paoli, A. (2022). The potential of digital ethnography for sensitive topics and hidden population. *Italian Sociological Review, 12*, 729–747.

Delli Paoli, A., & D'Auria, V. (2021). Digital ethnography: A systematic literature review. *Italian Sociological Review, 11*(4S), 243–267.

Delli Paoli, A., & Masullo, G. (2022). The desexualization of society. A digital ethnography on the asexual community, introduction to the special section. *Italian Journal of Sociology of Education, 14*(3), 153–172.

Kay, J. B. (2022). Abject desires in the age of anger: Incels, femcels and the gender politics of unfuckability. In *Imagining "We" in the Age of "I"*. Routledge, pp. 29–46.

Knight, S. (2019). *Facebook reportedly receives half a million revenge porn complaints each month*. Techspot, 18 /11.

Ling, R. (2022). *Femcels: Are they really the female equivalent of the incel? Master's thesis*. Simon Fraser University.

MacKinnon, C. (2006). *Are women human? And other international dialogues*. Cambridge, MA: Harvard University Press.

Mulvey, L. (1975). *Visual pleasure and narrative cinema. Screen, 16*(3), Autumn 1975, Pages 6–18.

Nagle, A., & Pirocchi, F. M. (2018). *Contro la vostra realtà: come l'estremismo del web è diventato mainstream*. Roma: LUISS University Press.

Patton, M. (1990). *Qualitative evaluation and research methods*. Beverly Hills, CA: Sage, pp. 169–186.

Pizzimenti D., Penna A. (2024). Excluded. A Digital Ethnographic Investigation on the Femcel

Community. Italian Sociological Review, ISSN 2239-8589. DOI: 10.13136/v14i10S.729 2024,

14(10S), pp. 765 – 786.

Pizzimenti D., & Pasciuto, F. (2022). *Un'analisi netnografica sul fenomeno dell'hate speech nella manosfera italiana*. Metis. Ricerche di sociologia, psicologia e antropologia della comunicazione, vol. XXIX, 1-2.

Priulla G. (2023). *La violenza simbolica in Pluralismi. in Riflessioni su corpi, politiche e rappresentazioni di genere*, (a cura di AA.VV.). Mimesis.

Statista. (2019). *Percentage of U.S. adults who use Reddit as of February 2019*. Statista.Com. https://www.statista.com/statistics/261770/share-of-us-internet-users-who-use-reddit-by-ethnicity/

Sumiala, J., & Tikka, M. (2020). Digital ethnographers on the move – An unexpected proposal. *Journal of Digital Social Research*.

Sunstein, C. R. (2017). *#Republic: Divided democracy in the age of social media*. Princeton and Oxford: Princeton University Press [trad. it (2017). *#Republic. com. La democrazia nell'epoca dei social media*, Il Mulino, Bologna].

The Economist, Intelligence Unit. (2021). *Measuring the prevalence of online violence against women*.

Turkle, S. (2019). *Insieme ma soli. Perché ci aspettiamo sempre più dalla tecnologia e sempre meno dagli altri*. Codice Edizioni [ed. or. (2011). *Alone together. Why we expect more from technology and less from each other*, Hackett Book Group].

van Dijck, J., Poell, T., & De Wall, M. (2018). *The platform society: Public values in a connectivity world*. Oxford: Oxford University Press [trad. It. (2019), *Platform Society: Valori pubblici e società connessa*, Guerini e Associati, Milano].

Wolf, N. (2022). (a cura di Gancitano, M. e Guerra, J.). *Il mito della bellezza*, edizioni Tlon [ed. or. 1990. *The Beauty Mith*].

Giuseppe Masullo and Marianna Coppola

Misgendering and transgender women: Between minority stress, resistance, and embedded imaginary

Abstract: The approach to gender-based violence highlights the need to examine it as a phenomenon not limited to women, but one that extends to all those categories of people (including transgender and/or non-binary individuals, etc.) who are discriminated against, oppressed, and excluded due to their gender identity and expression. In recent years, significant attention has been paid to microaggressions phenomena in digital environments that negatively impact the psychological well-being of those who experience them. Starting from a study conducted on a sample of transgender women, the essay highlights how digital environments prove to be useful contexts for performing the elective gender, but also environments in which old and new forms of oppression are evident. Among those less explored by Italian and international research, misgendering is understood as a discursive practice enacted by "digital haters" with the aim of denying the chosen and expressed gender of transgender individuals. Through in-depth interviews, the research examines the discursive strategies that these women employ to resist/justify misgendering, illustrating a typology of such reactions based on the main identified dimensions of meaning. It emerges how this violent and discriminatory practice is the result of a gendered and heteronormative culture that transgender people question in their attempt to self-determine. Furthermore, the results show how some of the interviewees develop ambivalent and contradictory feelings towards hate speech: while on one hand, it is condemned as an expression of widespread homotransphobia on the web, on the other hand, it is described as a test to validate their degree of passing for normal, understood as the ability to pass as a "cisgender" woman to others. This finding suggests that traditional gender models associated with femininity continue to influence the imagery of transgender women, and the degree of dissatisfaction and frustration resulting from the difficulty of adequately reaching and performing these "embedded" and therefore idealized models.

Introduction: New perspectives for the analysis of gender-based violence and discrimination

The approach to gender-based violence initiated during the 1995 United Nations Beijing Conference, highlights the need to examine gender-based violence as a phenomenon not limited solely to women but extending its focus to all those individuals (including transgender and/or non-binary individuals, etc.) who are oppressed and/or excluded due to their gender identity, expression, and non-heteronormative sexual orientation. On one hand, the approach to GBV empha-sizes the devastating effects of oppressive patriarchal practices, while on the other hand, it opposes the theory of the naturalness of normative heterosexuality and the male-female binary juxtaposition as the basis of gender-based violence (Collins, 2008). These dichotomous logics that pool together differences into the man/woman binary – and, therefore, victim/perpetrator – are called into ques-tion precisely because they fail to recognize the heterogeneity of practices, pat-terns, and representations of gender-based violence and the variety of meanings in historically constructed contexts of domination (Corbisiero & Nocenzi, 2022).

This approach considers how gender-based violence is (re)produced through a mechanism that Bourdieu (1998) calls symbolic violence, which renders invisible the inequalities and asymmetries in which violence is situated. This mechanism also conceals the arbitrariness of the gender social order, which is interpreted in a convergent manner and perceived as obvious and inevitable by both men and women.

Expanding the focus to include categories considered as "non-standard" underscores the socially constructed nature of gender, the outcome of processes that, reproduce the gender order while, at the same time, engaging with unprec-edented processes of subjectivization that challenge it (Butler, 1993). There is an increasing demand for recognition from individuals who oppose such a state of affairs, considered by many as incontrovertible. Simultaneously, the need to think of gender identity as a variable aspect of the person or as something that does not perfectly correspond to the gender assigned at birth is emerging as in the case of transgender people[1]. The latter, in particular, are often subject to forms of violence expressed through processes of discrimination and social exclusion, insofar as they most fundamentally challenge the heterosexual order that, as is well known, establishes a perfect alignment between biological sex, gender identity, and (heterosexual) sexual orientation.

Today, the approach to GBV is also enriched by the spread of intersectional and postcolonial feminist perspectives, which allow attention to be focussed not only on the violent and discriminatory practices of men towards transgender

---

1   The term transgenderism describes the condition of individuals who experience an incongruence between their perceived gender and the gender assigned at birth accord-ing to their biological sex, leading to extreme discomfort, prompting them to undertake phenotypic, social, and legal alignment with the chosen gender (Valerio, 2001; Valerio et al., 2013).

women – albeit influenced by an approach that directly links transgenderism and deviance – but also on all acts of violence that occur because of gender identity, whether extra- or intra-categorical (Hill Collins, 2019). The former include forms of psychological, verbal, and material violence, as well as discrimination experienced by transgender women, for example, from cisgender women. The latter include violence perpetrated by other transgender women and more broadly within the diverse LGBTQ+ world.

The essay, based on research conducted on a sample of transgender women, highlights a form of violence that has been little explored by Italian and international research: misgendering, understood as a discursive practice – in some cases, a veritable form of hate speech – aimed at denying the gender expressed by transgender individuals (Coppola & Masullo, 2023, 2024).

Through biographical interviews (Bichi, 2002), the research examines the discursive strategies employed by these women in attempting to resist misgendering, the negative emotions they experience, and how these intentional and unintentional practices of disavowal impact the choices about the transition process itself. Considering the centrality of this journey to the level of perceived health, which will be better highlighted in the next section, the latter is often compromised by the discrimination and various forms of social exclusion experienced by transgender individuals in their social and relational lives (Punziano et al., 2022).

Minority stress and well-being of transgender individuals

The health of transgender individuals is a topic that has been relatively understudied in sociological research. The few existing studies have focussed on issues such as sexually transmitted diseases and sexual behaviours within a purely epidemiological framework, overlooking a wide range of equally important cultural and social variables (Masullo & Rinaldi, 2022).

A tradition of studies more aligned with cognitive and social psychology, using the concept of minority stress, has highlighted the close relationship between personal and social acceptance, on the one hand, and psychological well-being on the other (Scandurra et al., 2017). By adopting a perspective that frames the needs of a patient within the context of their psychological and relational characteristics, it shows that the health of individuals belonging to a stigmatized category, such as transgender people, must necessarily take into consideration the extent to which violence and discrimination affect the self-esteem, self-confidence, and perceived well-being of those who experience them (*ibid.*).

Lingiardi (2018) and Meyer (2003) have identified three interconnected dimensions that are mutually self-reinforcing in the construction and consolidation of minority stress: (a) experiences of discrimination and hostility related to one's non-normative gender identity and sexual orientation; (b) the perception of social stigma associated to the LGBTQ+ population; (c) the presence and consolidation of internalized hom/transphobia.

These foundational aspects of minority stress, when applied to the transgender population, take on specific characteristics. For example, transgender individuals frequently experience homo-transphobic attacks in multiple contexts of daily life, including the workplace, school, and often in service environments such as healthcare.

The perception of stigma for transgender individuals involves a level of vigilance regarding the fear (and subsequent discomfort) of not being identified with their gender (and, therefore, misgendered), being incorrectly identified (for example, being mistaken for homosexual individuals), or being associated with the world of prostitution and deviance (and thus with the negative stereotypes surrounding transgender people). Scientific literature has highlighted a direct proportionality between the perception of social rejection and the level of alertness and sensitivity to the environment, with consequent repercussions on the general and specific well-being of LGBTQ+ individuals (Strain et al., 2010; Skagerberg et al., 2013).

Transgender individuals with high levels of internalized homo-transphobia also display low self-esteem, poor self-acceptance, intolerance, and closure towards the LGBTQ+ community, up to severe forms of self-loathing and social isolation

Many transgender individuals, due to the aforementioned processes of stigmatization and discrimination related to either homo/trans-negativity or internalized homo/transphobia, give up on experiencing and living their feelings and sexuality (Masullo & Coppola, 2022).

Alongside these factors, transgender individuals place central importance on their psychological well-being on the alignment between their inner selves and their outward appearance, which directly relates to how they are socially identified. Being recognized by others according to their gender identity is not only crucial for their self-esteem but also for their overall perceived well-being, understood as the result of processes that involve both bodily and socio-relational dimensions. In a society dominated by heteronormative and cisnormative models, many potential opportunities expose transgender individuals to stigmatization and social discrimination. Additionally, transgender individuals are among the main victims of physical and verbal violence and hate speech, resulting from processes of homo/transphobia that pervade multiple relational spheres, including digital ones

As mentioned earlier, such occasions occur not only outside the transgender community but also within it, as highlighted by a recent study (Coppola & Masullo, 2023) examining the centrality of cis/hetero-normative models within the trans subculture as key requirements for self-acceptance and acceptance of and by others (transnormativity). Therefore, experiencing misgendering within the transgender community itself, especially towards those who exhibit, for example, a low "passing" (meaning the ability of transgender individuals to be perceived as cisgender individuals) is not uncommon.

Research design

Intending to explore how transgender women respond to the experience of misgendering in online environments, the research examined a sample of 20 transgender women aged between 18 and 23, residing in various areas in Italy, and interviewed online. The sample was selected using the snowball technique, whereby participants were contacted based on referrals from those already interviewed, who indicated friends and acquaintances willing to participate in the research.

The questions that guided the research are:

RQ1: How frequently do transgender women experience episodes of misgendering? And in what contexts?

RQ2: When this happens, what kind of emotions do they experience and how do these episodes affect minority stress?

RQ3: What reactions do women take to limit, justify, or resist misgendering both symbolically and behaviourally?

RQ4: If and how these episodes affect the transition process, determining choices and imaginary.

Utilizing the full potential of the biographical approach, the research administered a series of questions to 20 AMAB (assigned male at birth) women aged 18–25 residing in various areas of the country. These questions aimed at reconstructing and tracing these episodes from early childhood – when transgender women began to experience forms of identity and body dysphoria towards their assigned gender –throughout the transition process (just begun or in progress, since, as we will see below, it can never be said to be definitively concluded).

Misgendering transgender women: Phases and contexts

The analysis of the interviews has highlighted how the phase of the gender affirmation journey that transgender women are undergoing significantly influences their evaluation of misgendering.

Specifically, substantial differences emerged between an instance of misgendering experienced in the "Pre-T" phase, *i.e.* before starting hormone replacement therapy, compared to those experienced after a phenotypic adjustment and change in official documents and a phenotypic adjustment.

In the early stages of the gender affirmation journey, misgendering is seen as "normal" and, therefore, justified by transgender women because in the absence of phenotypic changes or even a "medical certification" there are few elements to attest to the new identity. Conversely, in the later stages, especially after obtaining legal recognition, it takes on a more complex meaning. In their opinion, it reflects the level of societal acceptance of issues related to identity self-determination or, more broadly, LGBTQ+ rights.

> *If I have to think about the phenomenon of misgendering, yes it does change a lot along the way. In the beginning it is normal, you experience it as even natural: you are not yet a woman, so what do you expect! But in the later stages, when you have started the process and your body, your image clearly reflects femininity, and you are misgendered, I see it as a blatant attempt to offend you, to denigrate the transgender person (V., 19, Rome).*

However, it seems that the context in which misgendering takes place plays an important role: the family or more formal and institutional contexts.

In the former case, misgendering is experienced by transgender women as something that is justified or mitigated by the difficulty of "rewriting family relationships" that, before the gender affirmation journey, revolved around a different arrangement of gender relations:

> *Of course, things have changed since starting hormone therapy. With the change in my appearance, it's more difficult to make mistakes, although she still does, especially when she gets angry, it is as if when she lets go she finds it easier to make mistakes (S., 20, Rome).*

Conversely, in institutional contexts, passing plays a central role, as Masullo and Coppola point out (2023). Here, the greater the passing, the lower the likelihood of experiencing misgendering. In any case, it is in more formal and institutional contexts that misgendering is experienced as a deliberate form of violence, thus increasing minority stress. For example, from an interview, it emerged that misgendering is not uncommon in healthcare services even in the presence of a high level of passing, especially if there has not yet been an adjustment of documents reflecting one's gender identity.

She kept calling me by my old name, even though she was face to face with a full-fledged woman, and when I pointed this out to her, the nurse said: "Listen, I can't do anything about it, on the documents you are a man!" (T. 24, Rome)

Misgendering: Between adaptation and resilience strategies

The emotions experienced by transgender women when they face misgendering are diverse and often conflicting. They can feel disheartened, disappointed, angry, or even desperate, especially when they believe they will never "pass" as a cisgender woman. This aspect is linked to how traditional gender models associated with femininity continue to influence transgender women's imaginary and their level of dissatisfaction and frustration resulting from the difficulty of achieving and performing them adequately.

In several interviews, it emerged that this lack of "social recognition" generates insecurity and symptoms typical of minority stress, such as social anxiety, and even forms of isolation to avoid feeling exposed and judged by others.

I remember that I didn't go out, I avoided everyone, especially at the beginning. My anxiety skyrocketed, I was so worried that someone might insult me, and call me a man, or a faggot. It was a horrible period (V. 19, Rome)

Internalized transphobia (as a cause of minority stress) often leads individuals to conceal their transgender history, especially in the early stages of the transition process (termed "undercovering"). In this case, misgendering is experienced as something negative and destabilising because it makes gender incongruence and belonging to a marginalized category visible and socially explicit.

At first, I tried to hide my condition, both as a homosexual guy and then with my gender incongruence (S., 21, Rome)

Alongside undercovering, the interviews highlighted how transgender women implement different coping strategies aimed at "performing" their gender identity by conforming to the predominant hetero-cisnormative models proposed and embraced by mainstream society

One way of reacting to the prevailing models – the cis/hetero-normative ones – is termed the *conforming process*, which involves transgender women attempting to modify certain phenotypic aspects and gender expressions as much as possible to align with the dominant model of femininity proposed by society. Here, misgendering can take on conflicting and somewhat paradoxical meanings: on the one hand, it may be seen as an offence; on the other hand, it is a means of obtaining feedback on one's social recognition. Regardless of the attributed meaning, these situations produce and exacerbate the stress of misgendered people

I know I am an ugly woman. I'm stuck with these shoulders, this face. I don't want to be seen as a trans woman, even though I know it is difficult. So, I spend a lot of time trying to improve or hide everything that might indicate that I used to be a guy. What does misgendering mean to me? It's confirmation that I need to improve and work on my body. If I'm misgendered, it means that I still don't pass as a woman (L., 22, Frosinone).

Experiencing the frustration inevitably caused by misgendering can often have negative effects on both psychological and physical health. The sample of women interviewed also revealed a tendency towards "overcovering", typical of transgender women who are dysfunctionally obsessed with surgery and cosmetic treatments to correspond as closely as possible to the "incorporated" gender model. Often, this tendency leads to choices that can pose health risks, such as buying drugs used for gender-affirming hormone replacement therapy on the black market, as well as negatively impact the doctor-patient relationship, with requests for increasingly massive doses

I know of friends of mine who did not wait for the typical timeline of hormone therapy and turned to older trans women, those who are experienced and outside the mainstream. I know of a girl who, in a few months, had changed her appearance and was taking a dose 4 times stronger than mine, all to look 100% female (D. 19, Florence).

Other reactions or agency strategies are instead the product of more mature stages of the transition process, particularly the processing of internalized transphobia and social anxiety, resulting from long meetings and sessions with psychologists or a history of activism within LGBTQ+ communities. In this case, transgender women emancipate themselves from the dominant model of femininity, proposing new, alternative models, as the result not only of elaboration of internalized transphobia but also the ability to distance themselves from stereotyped visions classically associated with both mainstream femininity and the more specific world of transgender individuals. In such cases, the rejection of models is linked to a broader vision that conceives misgendering as a typical form of genderist and heteronormative oppression and thus a trait of a society that expresses a broader homo-trans negativity

How do I react to misgendering? By providing education and information. Many people need to be educated and corrected to bring them up to date. We have a social and collective imperative in this, because every time we let misgendering or deadnaming pass, we harm the cause of the transgender community; therefore, we must always emphasise that this is a form of oppression, like so many others in contemporary society (C., 21, Rome).

Conclusions: Misgendering as a gender feedback process

From a sociological perspective, social recognition is the fundamental prerequisite for communicating an identity. Essential to being recognized is to be visible

(McLaren et al., 2021; Di Gregorio, 2019). Gender visibility is an aspect widely overlooked in sociological research on these topics. It is forgotten that "gender" is not only something that individuals self-attribute, but is also an effect of hetero-attribution, of how gender is interpreted by others based on the gender models prevalent in the collective imagination (Butler, 1993).

The visibility of one's gender is affirmed through the body – whose features refer to the two prevailing genders, male and female – through gender expression – wearing clothing corresponding to the gender of affiliation. However, it can also be revealed through personal documents (*e.g.* ID cards) or be disclosed – especially in correspondence with prevalent social stereotypes – through cultural interests, as well as social circles. Every aspect of a person, therefore, can refer to the gender to which they feel they belong and simultaneously to the gender others attribute to them based on those characteristics, often linked to stereotypes. In this research, visibility refers to the elective gender, which for transgender individuals is harmoniously constructed by referring to one or more of the aspects mentioned. For them, the research results show, the visibility of one's gender constitutes a boundary, which assumes a different meaning depending on the stage of the transition process. Initially, visibility can be a problem that exacerbates minority stress, insofar as being visible in one's dysphoric characteristics means being associated with stigmatized categories; subsequently, however, it becomes an opportunity, since the correct communication of one's gender is part of the social affirmation process of the gender itself.

The stories collected in this research are certainly stories of transition, but they can also be defined as stories of visibility and communication of one's gender, which transgender individuals desire to affirm not only privately but especially publicly. There are phases in which gender is understated, almost suppressed and denied, in favour of the one assigned at birth, alternating with phases in which it is practically exhibited (gender euphoria).

Misgendering thus assumes a dynamic rather than static connotation for the gender affirmation process, allowing to highlight the role that social recognition plays in these processes, both in negative terms (as a genuine act of violence) and in affirmative terms (as confirmation of the adequacy of one's gender identity). The research thus allows us to explore the role of misgendering within what can be defined as a gender feedback process.

From the life stories collected, we can identify four phases of this process, each corresponding to a different symbolic construction and function of misgendering (See figure below).

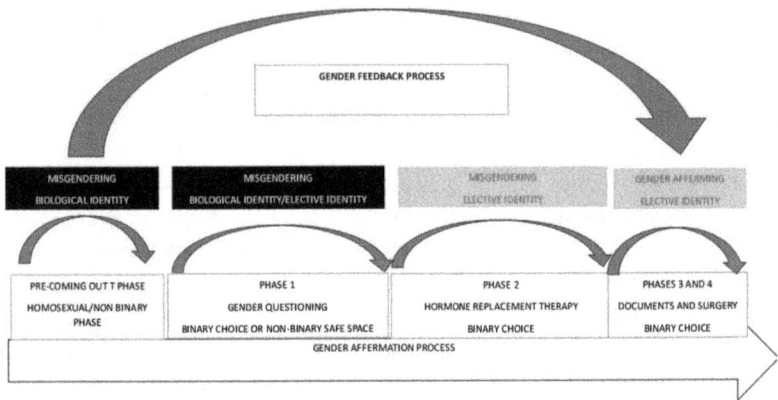

| GENDER FEEDBACK PROCESS |

| MISGENDERING | MISGENDERING | MISGENDERING | GENDER AFFIRMING |
| BIOLOGICAL IDENTITY | BIOLOGICAL IDENTITY/ELECTIVE IDENTITY | ELECTIVE IDENTITY | ELECTIVE IDENTITY |

PRE-COMING OUT T PHASE	PHASE 1	PHASE 2	PHASES 3 AND 4
HOMOSEXUAL/NON BINARY PHASE	GENDER QUESTIONING	HORMONE REPLACEMENT THERAPY	DOCUMENTS AND SURGERY
	BINARY CHOICE OR NON-BINARY SAFE SPACE	BINARY CHOICE	BINARY CHOICE
GENDER AFFERMATION PROCESS

Source: author's elaboration

In the first phase, known as the pre-coming phase, the individual lives in all social contexts with their biological identity. In this phase, misgendering takes on a negative connotation, which tends to highlight their non-belonging to the hetero-cisnormative model. Here, individuals tend to deny their gender incongruence, often defining themselves as a particularly effeminate homosexual person, or choosing to self-identify as non-binary, using non-binary identity as a safe space for identity definition (Scandurra et al., 2019).

The second is the phase of gender questioning and the beginning of psychological consultations to start the gender adjustment process; it also coincides with the coming-out phase. Transgender women in this phase generally make a binary identity choice and misgendering assumes a control and monitoring function to probe and assess the openings or closures of relational contexts on their choice of transitioning to a new gender.

The third phase coincides with the gender affirmation process where hormone replacement therapy begins and transgender women make a binary identity self-determination choice, accompanied by the first phenotypic and gender expression changes. Here, misgendering plays a central role in the journey, as it is perceived as feedback to obtain social confirmation of the adequacy and capability of the individual to perform the chosen gender.

A final phase that we can define as gender affirming corresponds to changing documents and conversion surgery, in which misgendering is experienced as further evidence of the ability to adequately perform the reference gender models. As in previous phases, social recognition plays an essential role, and much depends on the ability of transgender individuals to process reference models, and on overcoming minority stress (internalized transphobia, social anxiety, etc.). thus, misgendering can, on the one hand, be conceived as an additional form of "stress" leading to extreme and risky health choices – to the extent that transgender women continue to attach importance to these models and feel ashamed for not being sufficiently capable of performing them. On the other hand, it can push towards the affirmation of a more authentic gender, the result of a more realistic and personal elaboration of identity, the latter aspect positively reverberating on minority stress, leading to greater self-esteem and, therefore, a greater perceived psychological well-being.

References

Bichi, R. (2002). *L'intervista biografica. Una proposta metodologica*. Milano: Vita e Pensiero.

Bourdieu, P. (1998). *La domination masculine*. Paris: Seuil [trad. it. Il dominio maschile, Milano: Feltrinelli,].

Butler, J. (1993). *Bodies that matter: On the discursive limits of sex*. London-New York: Routledge.

Collins, R. (2008). *Violence. A micro-sociological theory*. Princeton: Princeton University Press.

Coppola, M., & Masullo, G. (2023). La negazione identitaria come forma di violenza: il misgendering nei confronti delle persone transgender nei contesti di vita. *AG-About Gender – International Journal of Gender Studies, 12*(24), 263–292.

Coppola, M., & Masullo, G. (2024). Discrimination and hate speech among transgender individuals in a online community: between passing and transnormativity. In E. Gualda (ed.), *Teorías de la conspiración y discursos de odio en línea en la sociedad de las plataformas Comparación de pautas en las narrativas y redes sociales sobre COVID-19, inmigrantes, refugiados, estudios de género y personas LGTBIQ+*. Madrid: Dykinson, ISBN 978-84-1170-913-2, pp. 273–288.

Corbisiero, F., & Nocenzi, M. (a cura di) (2022). *Manuale di educazione al genere e alla sessualità*. Milano: Milano.

Di Gregorio, L. (2019). *Oltre il corpo: la condizione transgender e transessuale*. Milano: FrancoAngeli.

Hill Collins, P. (2019). *Intersectionality as critical social theory*. Durham and London: Duke University Press.

Lingiardi, V., & McWilliams, N. (a cura di) (2018). *Manuale Diagnostico Psicodinamico*, seconda edizione (PDM-2). Milano: Raffaello Cortina Editore.

Masullo, G., & Coppola, M. (2022). Transgender couples' lives: Between specificity, the need for normalization, and new forms of social discrimination. In B. Gilley & G. Masullo (Eds.), *Non-binary family configurations: Intersections of Queerness and Homonormativity* (pp. 93–108). Berlin: Springer Nature.

Masullo, G., & Rinaldi, C. (2022). Introduzione. In G. Masullo e C. Rinaldi (a cura di), *La Salute delle persone LGBTQI+: fra invisibilità, stigmatizzazione e segnali di empowerment*. Rivista "Salute e Società", XXI, n. 2. Milano: FrancoAngeli editore, XXI, pp. 5–8.

McLaren, J. T., Bryant, S., & Brown, B. (2021). See me! Recognize me! An analysis of transgender media representation. *Communication Quarterly, 69*(2), 172–191.

Meyer, I. H. (2003). Prejudice as stress: Conceptual and measurement problems. *American Journal of Public Health, 93*, 262–265.

Punziano, G., Coppola, M., & Avellino, A. (2022). Benessere, transizioni di genere e capability approach: un'indagine esplorativa sulla popolazione T. *Salute e Società*, vol. 2. pp. 131–148.

Scandurra, C., Amodeo, A, Valerio, P., Bochicchio, V., & Frost, D. M. (2017). Minority stress, resilience, and mental health: A study of Italian transgender people. *Journal of Social Issues, 73*(3), 563–585.

Scandura, C., Mezza, F., & Bochicchio, V. (2019). Individui non-binary e gender queer: Una review critica su salute, stigma e risorse. *La camera blu, 21*, 1–57.

Skagerberg, E., Davidson, S., & Carmichael, P. (2013). Internalizing and externalizing behaviors in a group of young people with gender dysphoria. *International Journal of Transgenderism, 14*, 105–112.

Strain, J. D., & Shuff, I. M. (2010). Psychological well-being and level of outness in a population of male-to-female transsexual women attending a national transgender conference. *International Journal of Transgenderism, 12*(4), 230–240.

Valerio, P. (a cura di) (2001). *Il transessualismo. Saggi psicoanalitici*. Milano: FrancoAngeli.

Valerio, P., Vitello, R., Romeo, R., Fazzari, P. (2013). *Figure dell'identità di genere. Uno sguardo tra psicologia, clinica e discorso sociale*. Milano: Franco Angeli.

Stefano Poli, Paola Giannoni and Giada Moretti

Violence against older women in Italy: Understanding the scope and possible interventions

Abstract: Older people abuse refers to physical abuse as well as psychological, sexual, financial, pharmaceutical abuse and neglect, and often occurs within a relationship where there is an expectation of trust (Rudatis, 2020). The WHO estimates that, in 2022, 15.7 % of people aged 60 and over were affected by abuse, with a greater risk for older women (Spangler & Brandl, 2007). This appears particularly relevant in the Italian context, where there is a notable trend in population ageing. However, despite available data indicating a widespread occurrence of older people abuse in the Italian context, phenomenon remains largely underestimated (Badenes-Ribera et al., 2021) and lacks a specific legal and policy framework (Melchiorre et al., 2014). In this regard, the paper aims to provide new evidence on violence against older women in Italy, by presenting a survey carried out in Genoa, a metropolitan urban context characterized by a significant population of older people, investigating episodes of violence and/or discrimination on a sample of 1,354 over 65 community-dwelling residents. Our results reveal that 23.3 % of respondents reported to have experienced episodes of violence, with distinct patterns emerging between older men and women. Especially for female respondents, regardless of old age group, social interaction combined with solitary family conditions and lack of services in deprived contexts represent predictive factors of higher risk of experiencing violence. In conclusion, our study underlines the need for a multidimensional perspective to understand patterns of violence against older women, a remarkable issue that is expected to increase with the rapidly increasing population of older people.

Keywords: older women, older people abuse, violence, gender, victimization

Introduction

The World Health Organization (WHO) has defined older people abuse as "a single or repeated action, or a lack of appropriate action, that takes place within any relationship in which an expectation of trust develops and causes harm or pain to the older person", identifying female gender as a major risk factor, alongside age-related prejudices like ageism. These prejudices contribute to the perpetuation of cultural stereotypes deeply rooted in society and allowing a certain "tolerance of violence" against older people (WHO, 2022). According to WHO estimates as of 2022, 15.7 % of people aged 60 and over have been experienced instances of senior abuse and approximately one out of six have experienced some form of abuse in community settings in recent years, with older women being at higher risk.

Only some of these cases are officially reported, underscoring a broader scope and an escalating prevalence also due to the increasing population of older people. Consequently, methodological issues arise in comprehensively studying the phenomenon, because of the difficulty of detection caused by the underestimation of the problem. Baker et al. (2016) emphasized the existence of discrepancies within the available evidence, particularly in evaluating the efficacy of interventions designed to address older people abuse, as well as the need to produce high-quality scientific studies, with adequate statistical representativeness to estimate the extent of the phenomenon more precisely.

Women are generally more susceptible to experiencing violence and abuse, although the prevalence of this tendency may vary depending on the specific type of abuse (Biggs et al., 2009). International literature underscores the existence of both structural and socio-cultural risk factors that contribute to violence against older women. Notably, gender-specific research on violence against women tends to concentrate on the 15–49 age group, neglecting a comprehensive exploration of patterns and types of violence against women aged 50 and above (Meyer et al., 2020). In relationships where older female victims experience abuse, power dynamics replicate those imposed on younger women, frequently resulting in subordination or financial exploitation (Spangler & Brandl, 2007). The significantly increased risk of senior abuse is linked to the socio-economic and financial characteristics of family members caring for older relatives (Lino et al., 2019). Some studies have highlighted that women who take care of their older family members may be at a higher risk of becoming perpetrators of abuse (Melchiorre et al., 2017). Furthermore, most studies predominantly focus on hospital and healthcare contexts, neglecting research on community settings, despite the widespread occurrence of domestic violence experienced by older women (Yon et al., 2019).

The previous issues appear particularly relevant in the Italian context, characterized by significant population ageing. In 2022, individuals aged 65 and above represent 23.8 % of the overall population, of which 56.1 % are older women, outnumbering the male counterpart, especially in older age classes, and rising to 59.4 % within the over-75 group (source: ISTAT data). However, the prolonged lifespan of females seems to be linked to a higher risk of isolation, depression, and chronic health conditions compared to men (Melchiorre et al., 2014). Additionally, older women often contend with unsatisfactory living conditions, related to lower socioeconomic status and educational attainment (Donati, 2010), thereby reflecting increased vulnerability to experiencing violence alongside rising inequalities (Rudatis, 2020). Furthermore, the vulnerability of older people seems to have exacerbated during the COVID-19 emergency (Shimoni, 2020), rendering them more prone to maltreatment. Data at national level regarding accident and emergency ward attendances in hospital of women over 65 due to violence indicate an increase from a value of 2.8 per 10,000 in 2017–2019 to 3.2 per 10,000 attendances in 2020–2021 among Italian older women. For foreign older women, the corresponding figures rose from a value of 4.5 per 10,000 in 2017–2019 to 5.4 per 10,000 attendances in 2020–2021 (source: Italian Ministry of Health on EMUR data).

Further research on violence against older women is needed, but studies in the Italian context have already highlighted the critical role of a gender approach in understanding related risk factors. Donati (2010) emphasizes that only through a gender-sensitive perspective can imbalances and injustices within family relationships be unveiled. These issues often occur in the private sphere, where patriarchal history has tended to normalize abuse and violence against women, also influenced by demographic and social variables. Sgritta and Deriu's study (2009) identifies marital status, economic precariousness, and health problems as significant risk factors for older people in Italy. They note that a part of the older population is often overlooked in studies due to social exclusion and withdrawal from private life. Offering a valuable contribution, Badenes-Ribera et al. (2021) examine the risk factors associated with maltreatment among older people, highlighting how caregivers and family members often emerge as primary perpetrators. Beriotto (2021) emphasizes that, alongside favourable health conditions, the structural support of an adequate community setting, and a dedicated legal framework are protective factors against violence for older individuals. Notably, better socioeconomic conditions are highlighted as protective factors, with the observation that older men, enjoying more privileged positions, are less susceptible to violence, while older women, experiencing greater marginalization, are at a higher risk of incurring violence.

Therefore, this paper aims to provide new evidence about violence against older people, with a specific focus on older women, by investigating possible episodes of suffered violence through a survey carried out in Genoa, a metropolitan urban area characterized by a significant population of older people. In the following sections, the methods and procedures used to realize the study will be described, the results of the research presented, and their implications discussed, in relation to existing knowledge in the field. The analysis will also explore the limitations of the study while suggesting directions for future research, by highlighting the need to adopt a multidimensional approach to understand patterns of violence against older women.

Method

The study was part of a larger research intervention («PRESTIGE – Partecipi e RESilienTi: Invecchiare a GEnova») about frailty among community-dwelling older people, developed between 2019 and 2020 by the University of Genoa, the Galliera Hospital of Genoa, and Auser Liguria with funding from the Carige Bank Foundation. The research, based in Genoa, Italy, included a sample of 1,354 individuals aged 65 and older, drawn from a population of 166,151 residents (as of January 2017) with a survey investigating the health conditions of older people from a multidimensional perspective (physical and cognitive status, social capital, professional experience, lifestyle, socioeconomic variables, etc.) and their social vulnerability, with a specific focus on episodes of violence experienced.

Such episodes represent the main dependent variable of the present study and are evaluated referring to possible aggression suffered by the respondents, reporting with a score of "1", if the respondent declared to have been victim in the last five years of any event such as theft, robbery, scams, physical assault, usury, or any other reported violence ("0", in case of any occurring episode).

The independent variables were considered as possible predictive or protective factors. Gender was considered in evaluations of any differences, particularly considering the major incidence of older women in chronic conditions among the frail population (Caroli & Weber-Baghdiguian, 2016). Age was considered in chronological terms, dividing the sample into two subgroups of respondents: aged 65–74 and over 75. The degree of disability was evaluated by assessing functional independence both in terms of activities of daily living (ADL) and instrumental activities of daily living (IADL), recoding a score of "1", indicating the presence of ADL or IADL impairments and of "0" for all respondents without an ADL or IADL deficit. These two domains were additionally considered by the SELFY-MPI scale (Pilotto et al., 2008; 2019) assessing frail conditions with a score ranging from 0.00 (minimum risk) and 1.00 (maximum mortality risk). Regarding the status domain, the level of education was assessed by classifying the reported educational qualifications according to the International Standard Classification of Education (ISCED), successively recoded in None/Compulsory school (ISCED 0–2), Apprentice/diploma (ISCED 3–4) and Bachelor/PhD (ISCED 5–6). Economic difficulties were observed on an ordinal scale ranging from "1 – struggling to make ends meet", "2 – spending everything earned and drawing on savings", "3 – spending everything earned", "4 – able to save something", "5 – able to save and invest something" (see Cesareo, 2007), successively recoding economic difficulties in "none" (previous modalities 4 and 5), "somewhat" (3) and serious (1 and 2). Affective states were assessed via the Positive and Negative Affect Scale (PANAS, see Watson et al., 1988). The relational dimension was evaluated by observing the number of persons in the household (living alone, two persons, three or more), the level of social disconnectedness, and of social network. To evaluate isolation, we adopted the Social Disconnectedness Scale (SDS), validated by Cornwell and Waite (2009). According to the authors, social disconnectedness can be defined by a lack of contact with others and a reduced and limited network, poor social involvement and low support due to scarce relationships both in terms of frequency and quality, inside and outside the household. Thus, social disconnectedness items were related to social network characteristics. A scale score of 0 indicates that the respondent provided the mean response for each of the included items. Positive scores indicate greater-than-average isolation, whereas negative scores indicate lower-than average isolation.

Lastly, we defined a set of variables within the agency and lifestyle domain (see Poli & Pandolfini, 2016), including: the level of cultural fruition (referred to staying informed, practicing cultural activities, hobbies and traveling); the overall satisfaction regarding services in the neighbourhood (green spaces, leisure and cultural activities, commercial and daily needs activities, transport, social and health care, safety); the technological fruition (use of mobile, PC, Internet, online payments, and debit and credit cards).

The relationships between episodes of violence experienced and all other aforesaid variables were preliminary observed in bi-variate crosstabs analysis, evaluating significance with Pearson chi-square values. Subsequently, a multivariate perspective was adopted, trough a logistic regression model (firstly, on the overall sample, and, successively, by gender) and a stepwise backward-selection method (likelihood-ratio test <0.2), to test the association between the dependent variable and all factors cited above.

Results: The emersion of different interpretative patterns of violence suffered by older women

Baseline characteristics of the study population by occurrence of episodes of violence suffered are summarized in Table 1.

Considering socio-demographic characteristics, our sample results quite equidistributional in terms of gender (55.8 % women vs 44.2 % men), slightly tending towards older groups (40.4 % young-old vs 59.6 % older-old) and reporting the presence of ADL deficit for 19.4 % of respondents, with a moderate/high risk of frailty on the SELFY-MPI scale for 15.6 % of cases (corresponding to the standard share of frail subjects in standard over 65s population, see Poli & Pandolfini, 2016). The level of education is prevalently lower (56.4 % vs 43.5 % reporting average/higher education), with about one over five (18.3 %) reporting major economic difficulties. Most of the sample lives with a partner (53.2 %), or alone (32.0 %), with a good level of social relationships (only 14.9 % reports a greater than average level of social disconnectedness and 26.7 % a lesser developed level of social network). Overall, levels of more or less positive/negative emotional attitudes measured on the PANAS scale seem to be equally distributed, although higher levels of negative emotional conditions rise among older women (38.6 for female vs 33.0 for male respondents). A total of 33.2 % refers to a higher level of satisfaction regarding services (with gender differences: 34.5 % for men vs 29.1 % for women) and 44.5 % reports higher levels of cultural fruition, even if most of the sample seems to suffer more digitally, with 55.9 % reporting a lower level of technological fruition.

Observing the main dependent variable, the final distribution of respondents resulted in 316 individuals (23.3 %) reporting episodes of violence experienced. The older age group, the presence of ADL deficits expressing actual frail conditions assessed with the level of SELFY MPI risk, the larger number of persons in a household, lower levels of social disconnectedness (indicating major social involvement), and negative emotional conditions assessed through PANAS scale, were all significantly associated with reported episodes of violence suffered. On the contrary, other variables, like level of education or economic difficulties, were not significantly associated according to the statistics. Furthermore, the gender dimension was not significantly associated with the occurrence of episodes of aggression, although older women reported slightly higher levels of violence suffered in proportion (23.7 % for female vs 22.9 % for male respondents).

The latter result led to a deeper exploration of the gender dimension by realizing distinct logistic regression models, both for the overall sample, and, separately, for male and female respondents, to better understand possible interpretative and predictive patterns of aggression suffered by older men and older women. Such logistic regression models are reported in Table 2.

Observing the logistic regression model for the overall sample (N=1.354), as mentioned, gender did not emerge as a statistically significant factor, and was excluded by the algorithm (along with the presence of IADL deficits, the level of SELFY-MPI risk, the level of education, the level of economic difficulties, the level of social disconnectedness, and the Ntiles of positive PANAS). Older age group (OR=0.72, 95 %, CI: 0.54–0.95), presence of ADL deficits (OR=0.68, 95 %,

CI: 0.49–0.95) and more people in the household (OR=0.74, 95 %, CI: 0.61–0.90) were significant protective factors against violence, while higher levels of negative emotional conditions in PANAS scale (OR=1.21, 95 %, CI: 1.03–1.42), lesser satisfaction regarding services (OR=0.86, 95 %, CI: 0.73–1.01), and more cultural fruition (OR=1.22, 95 %, CI: 1.04–1.42) emerged as predictive factors of occurred violence episodes.

However, replicating the algorithm separately according to gender resulted in different explicative factors.

When observing the logistic regression model interpreting episodes of violence experienced by older women, interestingly, the age factor disappeared from the model, and the presence of ADL deficits (OR=0.67, 95 %, CI: 0.45–1.00), along with a larger number of persons in the household (OR=0.46, 95 %, CI: 0.34–0.64) appeared as statistically significant protective factors, while higher levels of social network (OR=1.33, 95 %, CI: 0.99–1.77) and lower levels of satisfaction regarding services (OR=0.46, 95 %, CI: 0.34–0.64) resulted as predictive factors of higher risk.

On the contrary, as regards male respondents, older age reappeared as a protective factor (OR=0.56, 95 %, CI: 0.36–0.57), while higher levels of negative emotional conditions according to the PANAS scale, (OR=1.38, 95 %, CI: 1.09–1.75), and increasing levels of cultural and technological fruition (OR=1.25, 95 %, CI: 0.97–1.61, and OR=1.47, 95 %, CI: 0.93–2.33, respectively) described predictive factors of higher risk.

Table 1: Episodes of violence experienced by possible predictive factors (N=1,354).

		Reported episodes of violence experienced									χ^2 test p-value
		Count			% row			% columns			
		no	yes	total	no	yes	Total	no	yes	Total	
Overall sample		1,038	316	1,354	76.7	23.3	100.0	-	-	-	-
Gender	Female	577	179	756	76.3	23.7	100.0	55.6	56.6	55.8	0.74
	Male	461	137	598	77.1	22.9	100.0	44.4	43.4	44.2	
Age group	65–74 years old	438	109	547	80.1	19.9	100.0	42.2	34.5	40.4	0.01
	over 74 years old	600	207	807	74.3	25.7	100.0	57.8	65.5	59.6	

(*continued*)

Table 1: Continued

		Reported episodes of violence experienced									χ2 test
		Count			% row			% columns			p-value
		no	yes	total	no	yes	Total	no	yes	Total	
Presence of ADL deficits	No	853	239	1092	78.1	21.9	100.0	82.2	75.6	80.6	0.01
	Yes	185	77	262	70.6	29.4	100.0	17.8	24.4	19.4	
Presence of IADL deficits	No	12	2	14	85.7	14.3	100.0	1.2	0.6	1.0	0.42
	Yes	1,026	314	1340	76.6	23.4	100.0	98.8	99.4	99.0	
Level of SELFY MPI risk	Low	889	253	1142	77.8	22.2	100.0	85.6	80.1	84.3	
	moderate	83	46	129	64.3	35.7	100.0	8.0	14.6	9.5	0.00
	High	66	17	83	79.5	20.5	100.0	6.4	5.4	6.1	
Level of education	Low	584	180	764	76.4	23.6	100.0	56.3	57.0	56.4	
	average	329	98	427	77.0	23.0	100.0	31.7	31.0	31.5	0.97
	High	125	38	163	76.7	23.3	100.0	12.0	12.0	12.0	
Economic difficulties	None	661	188	849	77.9	22.1	100.0	63.7	59.5	62.7	
	average	195	62	257	75.9	24.1	100.0	18.8	19.6	19.0	0.32
	Major	182	66	248	73.4	26.6	100.0	17.5	20.9	18.3	
Number of persons in household	living alone	305	128	433	70.4	29.6	100.0	29.4	40.5	32.0	
	two persons	573	147	720	79.6	20.4	100.0	55.2	46.5	53.2	0.00
	three or more	160	41	201	79.6	20.4	100.0	15.4	13.0	14.8	
Level of social disconnected-ness	lower than average	174	75	249	69.9	30.1	100.0	16.8	23.7	18.4	
	average	703	194	897	78.4	21.6	100.0	67.7	61.4	66.2	0.01
	greater than average	161	47	208	77.4	22.6	100.0	15.5	14.9	15.4	
Level of social network	Lower	269	93	362	74.3	25.7	100.0	25.9	29.4	26.7	
	average	540	158	698	77.4	22.6	100.0	52.0	50.0	51.6	0.47
	Higher	226	65	291	77.7	22.3	100.0	21.8	20.6	21.5	
NTILES of positive PANAS	Lower	354	104	458	77.3	22.7	100.0	34.1	32.9	33.8	
	average	328	103	431	76.1	23.9	100.0	31.6	32.6	31.8	0.91
	Higher	356	109	465	76.6	23.4	100.0	34.3	34.5	34.3	
NTILES of negative PANAS	Lower	376	83	459	81.9	18.1	100.0	36.2	26.3	33.9	
	average	319	111	430	74.2	25.8	100.0	30.7	35.1	31.8	0.00
	Higher	343	122	465	73.8	26.2	100.0	33.0	38.6	34.3	

Table 1: Continued

		Reported episodes of violence experienced									χ2 test p-value
		Count			% row			% columns			
		no	yes	total	no	yes	Total	no	yes	Total	
Level of satisfaction regarding services	Lower	365	125	490	74.5	25.5	100.0	35.2	39.6	36.2	
	average	313	99	412	76.0	24.0	100.0	30.2	31.3	30.4	0.17
	Higher	358	92	450	79.6	20.4	100.0	34.5	29.1	33.2	
Level of cultural fruition	Lower	385	108	493	78.1	21.9	100.0	37.1	34.2	36.4	
	average	195	64	259	75.3	24.7	100.0	18.8	20.3	19.1	0.62
	Higher	458	144	602	76.1	23.9	100.0	44.1	45.6	44.5	
Level of tech. fruition	Lower	585	172	757	77.3	22.7	100.0	56.4	54.4	55.9	
	average/ higher	453	144	597	75.9	24.1	100.0	43.6	45.6	44.1	0.54

Table 2: Logistic regression models for episodes of violence experienced for overall sample and by gender.

		B	S.E.	Wald	df	Sig.	Exp(B)	95 % C.I.for EXP(B)	
								Lower	Upper
Overall sample (N=1354)	Age group	-0.328	0.144	5.143	1	0.023	0.721	0.543	0.957
	Presence of ADL deficits	-0.373	0.166	5.068	1	0.024	0.689	0.498	0.953
	Number of persons in household	-0.296	0.101	8.536	1	0.003	0.744	0.610	0.907
	NTILES of negative PANAS	0.195	0.080	5.884	1	0.015	1.216	1.038	1.423
	Level of satisfaction regarding services	-0.146	0.080	3.331	1	0.068	0.864	0.739	1.011
	Level of cultural fruition	0.200	0.079	6.300	1	0.012	1.221	1.045	1.427
	Constant	-0.769	0.349	4.864	1	0.027	0.464	-	-

(continued)

Table 2: Continued

		B	S.E.	Wald	df	Sig.	Exp(B)	95 % C.I.for EXP(B)	
								Lower	Upper
Female respondents (N=756)	Presence of ADL deficits	-0.391	0.204	3.692	1	0.055	0.676	0.454	1.008
	Number of persons in household	-0.758	0.164	21.338	1	0.000	0.468	0.340	0.646
	Level of social network	0.286	0.147	3.770	1	0.052	1.331	0.997	1.776
	Level of satisfaction regarding services	-0.190	0.108	3.108	1	0.078	0.827	0.670	1.021
	Constant	0.186	0.358	0.270	1	0.604	1.204	-	-
Male respondents (N=598)	Age group	-0.576	0.227	6.433	1	0.011	0.562	0.360	0.877
	NTILES of negative PANAS	0.326	0.121	7.267	1	0.007	1.385	1.093	1.755
	Level of cultural fruition	0.224	0.129	3.046	1	0.081	1.252	0.973	1.610
	Level of technological fruition	0.390	0.234	2.769	1	0.096	1.477	0.933	2.339
	Constant	-2.700	0.445	36.881	1	0.000	0.067	-	-

Discussion

Beyond the significant evidence of a widespread phenomenon of violence towards older people, our results clearly show different factors and possible patterns of violence experienced by senior male and female respondents, showing how older women are more likely to be at higher risk of suffering violence than men. The revelation that 23.3 % of respondents report to have suffered episodes of violence prompts a deeper exploration of associated factors. Age, ADL deficits, household size, social disconnectedness, and negative emotional conditions are found to be significant factors, emphasizing the multifaceted nature of the issue.

While existing literature suggests family members as potential perpetrators (Spangler & Brandl, 2007; Yon et al., 2019), showing that relatives, friends, and paid caregivers are often the most common emotional, psychological, and verbal abusers (Badenes-Ribera et al., 2021), our findings indicate a divergence. As a matter of fact, our results show evidence of how, in general, frail conditions experienced by individuals in larger families (with an implicit larger number of caregivers) provide some sort of protection, but pertaining to an older-old age group is not a protective factor for women. Similarly, while higher levels of agency and social interaction are predictive factors of possible violence for both genders, the risk of aggression increases for women in deprived contexts.

Logistic regression models reveal distinct patterns for each gender group. For older women, the absence of age as a factor suggests a greater influence of social dynamics. ADL deficits and larger household sizes act as protective factors, while social network strength and dissatisfaction with services emerge as predictive factors. Conversely, for older men, age remains a protective factor. Emotional conditions play a pivotal role, with higher negativity correlating with increased risk. Additionally, levels of cultural and technological fruition become notable predictive factors.

Therefore, one of the most interesting aspects is that, apart from disability deficits, older age is not a significant protective factor for senior women, unlike their male counterparts and contrary to expectations. Moreover, the rise of agency and interactivity with a larger social network, especially in more deprived contexts and when living independently (not simply "alone"), paradoxically increases the exposure to risk of suffering episodes of violence, without providing evidence of older age as a protective factor. Such results demonstrate a clear pattern of victimization by gender all through the life course. Only the presence of disability and a larger primary network represent effective protective factors. These latter factors are implicitly associated: community-dwelling seniors with disabilities probably live at home with almost one (or more) caregivers providing support and protection.

However, this latter aspect introduces one of the main limits of our study. Having observed a community-dwelling sample of older people, in our sample it is not possible to observe violence performed by professional caregivers in an institutionalized context. There may have been forms of domestic violence against our respondents by family or home caregivers, which may not have been reported via questionnaire due to the obtrusive nature of such topics. Future research efforts should aim to broaden the research frameworks to provide a comprehensive understanding of abuse against older adults. Furthermore, it would be useful to leverage the data from this survey for an in-depth exploration of potential forms of violence, particularly against older women.

Conclusions

The paper presents evidence highlighting the critical issue of violence against older individuals. It takes a dual perspective, examining the broader context of violence against seniors in general, while delving into specific patterns and risk factors across genders. The research highlights a pronounced discrimination against older women, shedding light on an often overlooked, underreported problem. Our results reflect a critical implication, especially when considered in tandem with a demographical scenario where a significant, increasing number of older women live alone, while maintaining independence and autonomy. This underlines the need to better explore these issues and their implications, particularly considering such an emerging, underreported phenomenon.

The study offers recommendations for policymakers, healthcare professionals, and community organizations to combat the concealed, underestimated violence against the most vulnerable victims within our society, paving the way for more targeted research and interventions in the field of older people abuse. This exploration could provide data to re-elaborate and update the legal and policy framework.

More support and intervention programs are needed for the complex, multidimensional typology of violent behaviors against seniors, especially older women, ranging from psychological to physical maltreatment, abuse, or abandonment. Such interventions should be accompanied by prevention strategies, proposing protective and support plans to prevent violence against older women, including awareness campaigns and education programs emphasizing mutual intergenerational exchange and solidarity. This includes services and specific programs available for older women who experience violence, providing greater accessibility for those who are more vulnerable.

Acknowledgements: While the article derives from several discussions between the authors, Giada Moretti is author of the section "Introduction"; Paola Giannoni is author of the sections "Methods" and "Results", and Stefano Poli is author of the sections "Discussion" and "Conclusions".

References

Badenes-Ribera, L., Fabris, M. A., & Longobardi, C. (2021). Elder mistreatment in an Italian population: Prevalence and correlates. *The International Journal of Aging and Human Development, 92*(1), 83–99.

Baker, P. R. A., Francis, D. P., Hairi, N. N., Othman, S., & Choo, W. Y. (2016). Interventions for preventing abuse in the elderly (Review). *Cochrane Database of Systematic Reviews 2016*, Issue 8. Art. No.: CD010321.

Beriotto, C. (2021). La violenza contro gli anziani: la percezione del fenomeno e l'impatto psicologico sugli operatori sanitari. *L'infermiere, 58*(4), 15–19.

Biggs, S., Manthorpe, J., Tinker, A., Doyle, M., & Erens, B. (2009). Mistreatment of older people in the United Kingdom: Findings from the first National Prevalence Study. *Journal of Elder Abuse & Neglect, 21*(1), 1–14.

Caroli, E., & Weber-Baghdiguian, L. (2016). Self-reported health and gender: The role of social norms. *Social Science & Medicine, 153*, 220–229.

Cesareo, V. (Ed.). (2007). *La distanza sociale. Una ricerca nelle aree urbane italiane*. Milano: FrancoAngeli.

Cornwell, E. Y., & Waite, L. J. (2009). Measuring social isolation among older adults using multiple indicators from the NSHAP study. *The Journals of Gerontology Series B: Psychological Sciences and Social Sciences, 64B*(S1), i38–i46. doi:10.1093/geronb/gbp037.

Donati, E. (a cura di), (2010). Indagine e studio sul tema della violenza nei confronti delle donne anziane, in La violenza contro le donne anziane: conoscere e sensibilizzare per prevenire. Un progetto contro la violenza a tutte le età, *Report Auser Regione Lombardia*, Pari e Dispari S.r.l.

Lino, V. T. S., Rodrigues, N. C. P., Lima, I. S. D., Athie, S., & Souza, E. R. D. (2019). Prevalence and factors associated with caregiver abuse of elderly dependents: The hidden face of family violence. *Ciencia & Saude Coletiva, 24*(1), 87–96. https://doi.org/10.1590/1413-81232018241.34872016

Melchiorre, M. G., Rosa, M. D., Barbabella, F., Barbini, N., Lattanzio, F., & Chiatti, C. (2017). Validation of the Italian version of the caregiver abuse screen among family caregivers of older people with Alzheimer's disease. *BioMed Research International*, 1–15. https://doi.org/10.1155/2017/3458372

Melchiorre, M. G., Penhale, B., & Lamura, G. (2014). Understanding elder abuse in Italy: perception and prevalence, types and risk factors from a review of the literature. *Educational Gerontology, 40*, 12.

Meyer, S. R., Lasater, M. E., & García-Moreno, C. (2020). Violence against older women: A systematic review of qualitative literature. *PLoS ONE, 15*(9).

Pilotto, A., Ferrucci, L., Franceschi, M., D'Ambrosio, L. P., Scarcelli, C., Cascavilla, L., Paris, F., Placentino, G., Seripa, D., Dallapiccola, B., & Leandro, G. (2008). Development and validation of a multidimensional prognostic index for one-year mortality from comprehensive geriatric assessment in hospitalized older patients. *Rejuvenation Research, 11*(1), 151–161. doi:10.1089/rej.2007.0569.

Pilotto, A., Veronese, N., Quispe Guerrero, K. L., Zora, S., Boone, A. L., Puntoni, M., Giorgeschi, A., Cella, A., Hidalgo, I. R., Pers, Y. M., Ferri, A., Fernandez, J. R. H., & Pisano Gonzalez, M. (2019). Development and validation of a self-administered multidimensional prognostic index to predict negative health outcomes in community-dwelling persons. *Rejuvenation Research, 22* (4), 299–305. doi: 10.1089/rej.2018.2103.

Poli, S., & Pandolfini, V. (2016). The incidence of social factors on elderly frailty evidences from a first methodological application of the Frail scale in Italy. *Bulletin of Sociological Methodology/Bulletin de Methodologie Sociologique*, May, 1–9. doi:10.1177/0759106316642720.

Rudatis, S. F. (2020). L'Assistente Sociale e la violenza contro le donne over 65. *I luoghi della cura*, 4.

Sgritta, G. B., & Deriu, F. (2009). *La violenza occulta. Violenze, abusi e maltratta-menti contro le persone anziane*, Edizioni Lavoro.

Shimoni, S. (2020). How coronavirus exposes the way we regard ageing and old people, in «The Conversation», published on March 2020, available online at: https://theconversation.com/howcoronavirus-exposes-the-way-we-regard-ageing-and-old-people-135134

Spangler, D., & Brandl, B. (2007). Abuse in later life: Power and control dynamics and a victim-centered response. *Journal of the American Psychiatric Nurses Association, 12*, 6.

Watson, D., Clark, L. A., & Tellegen, A. (1988). Development and valida-tion of brief measures of positive and negative affect: the PANAS scales. *Journal of Personality and Social Psychology, 54*(10), 63–70. doi: 10.1037/0022-3514.54.6.1063

World Health Organization. (2022). *Tackling abuse of older people: Five priorities for the United Nations decade of healthy ageing (2021–2030)*. World Health Organization. https://iris.who.int/handle/10665/356151.

Yon, Y., Mikton, C., Gassoumis, Z. C., & Wilber, K. H. (2019). The prevalence of self-reported elder abuse among older women in community settings: A sys-tematic review and meta-analysis. *Trauma, Violence, Abuse, 20*(2), 245–259.

Giuseppina Cersosimo

Conclusion

More than forty years ago Randall Collins drew attention to some elements which were bringing a change in the dictionary of violence: In our contemporary society, ferocious cruelty increase

> "(…) ascetic cruelty has had its ups and downs, cresting during periods of mobilized (…) it is no longer part of the dominant ceremonial order, (…) but at the same time, the dangers of callousness increase". (Collins, 1974, p. 440)

It was a warning of a progressive normalcy of the violence whose general and particular debate moved from previously basic historical, social and political observations (Arendt, 1970), to partial ones (Bell, 1960), being then linked to a new dictionary (Whiteson, 2007); and the further generalizations and in depth analyses (Sen, 2006; Žižek, 2008;). In this debate probably the variety investigated more and more fields in globalization, widening the interdisciplinary roots of the analysis (Gomez, Verdù, Gonzales-Megias, & Mendez, 2016) and paying growing attention to cultural historical long paths (Pinker, 2012). Our research, nurtured also from these studies, has however its reference research in that connected to violence against women. Actually these pages have double connection, one, more general, with historical forms of violence, its spread, and its statistical decrease during the twentieth century and another one which points out "the dangerous world" (Preble & Muller, 2014) and the continuous presence of violence in each space of the world as showed in Strand and Storey (2018) and the new implications about social and biological about women health (Gaudi et al., 2023).

Obviously this book, while not exhaustive of all the issues related to violence against women, has aimed to present some issues in terms of violence as a social determinant of health and well-being. To conclude, and without claiming to have closed or resolved such an important issue, it is necessary to consider how the various chapters of this book have highlighted how violence is transversal across generations, from girls to the elderly, and how not only the familiar, institutional environment, where gender inequality and the gender gap are still the product of a male tradition, but today also the natural environment, with its constant changes, and the digital-virtual environment, with its new forms of relationships, must be considered.

In fact, one of the most important impacts of climate change on human populations needs to be considered. Heat and drought disrupt agriculture and therefore the quantity and quality of food and water, leading to mass migration as populations seek better conditions for survival. Extreme global temperatures, droughts, floods and impacts on food and water disproportionately affect the health of women, who are most vulnerable to these impacts due to their social status and family responsibilities. Women and girls are at increased risk of sexual violence, sexual exploitation, abuse, trafficking and intimate partner violence as a result of displacement and vulnerability. The link between climate change and sexual and reproductive health and rights was recently summarized in the Women Deliver (2021) review. It identifies climate change as "non-gender neutral" because it reinforces social inequalities, with gender, sexuality, age, wealth, indigenousness and race all determining vulnerability to climate change.

Even the digital environments that have developed in our daily lives to facilitate and improve our quality of life, through technology that seems to make everything easier (Hilbert, 2013), more feasible, usable and convenient, end up being the essence of the malaise of women and girls who become targets of violence, aggression and shame, often leading them to become unwilling victims of the actions of others.

New research trajectories that correlate violence suffered and witnessed as a trace and epigenetic modification in the future of both the victim of violence and their sons and daughters should certainly not be overlooked.

It is necessary to rethink a history of social organization in which all women participate, together with the narratives in which we are protagonists and which lead back to that history, modifying the power relations, aware that the path of civilization follows a path that builds living and creative mediations (Muraro, 1991). We feel part of it, but the awareness that a path of equality and parity has not yet been fully achieved, is a premise that the new generations must be taught the value of differences and what each of us can express in the processes of relationships to contribute to the well-being of women and how many of them are still deprived of access to one of the fundamental rights due to conditions of economic, climatic, power deprivation, etc.

It is therefore useful that the approach experimented by many women in recent decades, of starting from oneself, an inseparable unity of body, culture and social practice, be transferred to younger people, in their education for citizenship and respect for diversity, and shared by men, with colleagues at work, in order to find new identities, new codes of communication, new forms of self-realization that avoid subordination to the logics of oppression. It is necessary to transform the confused impressions of the moral conscience into clear and precise notions

(Durkheim, 1912/1969), attributing new readings to social facts: thus, if education is capable of forming free citizens, the autonomous orientation of one's freedoms will also be free and make subjects free (Nussbaum, 2011).

References

Arendt, H. (1970). *On violence*. New York: Harcourt Brace & Co.

Bell, D. (1960). *The end of ideology*. New York: The Free Press

Collins, R. (1974). Three faces of cruelty: Towards a comparative sociology of violence. *Theory and Society, 1*(4), 415–440, http://doi.org/10.1007/BF00160802.

Durkheim, É. (1969). *L'educazione morale*. Torino: UTET.

Gaudi, S. e Falzarano L. (2023). Strategie multidisciplinari per prevenire e contrastare la violenza sulle donne: dai flussi di dati ai marcatori epigenetici Rapporto Istisan, Roma.

Gómez, J. M., Verdú, M., González-Megías, A., & Méndez, M. (2016). The phylogenetic roots of human lethal violence. *Nature, 538*(7624), 233–237, http://dx.doi.org/ 10.1038/nature19758.

Hilbert (2013) Muraro, L. (1991). *L'ordine simbolico della madre*. Roma: Editori Riuniti.

Pinker, S. (2012). *The better angels of our nature: A history of violence and humanity*. London: Penguin Books.

Preble, C. A., & Muller J. (2014). Threat Perception and U.S. National Security. Washington, D. C: Cato Institute

Nussbaum, M. C. (2011). *Creating capabilities. The human development approach*. Cambridge (Mass.) – London: The Belknap Press of Harvard University Press.

Sen, A. (2006). *Identity and violence. The illusion of destiny*. New York: W.W. Norton Company.

Strand, S. J. M., & Storey, J. E. (2018). Intimate partner violence in urban, rural, and remote areas: An investigation of offense severity and risk factors. *Violence Against Women, 25*(2), 188–207, https://doi.org/10.1177/1077801218766611.

Whiteson, L. (2007). *A terrible Beauty. An exploration of the positive role of violence in life, culture, and society*. Oakville: Mosaic Press.

Žižek, S. (2008). *Violence. Six sideways of reflection*. New York: Picado.

Notes on contributors

Valentina Amerighi is a specialized social worker, with a master's degree in Innovation and Social Work at the University of Padua. She works in a third sector organization dealing with marginalization and social inclusion. Since ever interested in understanding how social services and social workers, in collaboration with other services and other professionals, manage to respond to emergency and dramatic life events.

Daniela Belliti is PhD in political and social philosophy at the University of Milano-Bicocca. Her research fields are gender studies and the problems of peace and war. She is coordinator of the italian network UNIRE – Università in rete contro la violenza di genere. Her latest publications, *Cuori sacri. La solidarietà ai tempi del Covid* (Castelvecchi, Rome 2023) and *In cerca di pace. Parole, atti e discorsi sulla guerra in Ucraina e in Palestina* (GFEdizioni, Rome 2024)

Marianna Coppola PhD in Communication Sciences from the University of Salerno, Research Fellow in the Sociology of Cultural and Communicative Processes at the University of Molise. She works on gender and LGBTQ studies; media and social relations; digital death.

Giuseppina Cersosimo is full professor in Sociology at the University of Salerno. Her research interests include Sociological Theory, Qualitative Methods, Symbolic Interactionism, and Sociology of Health and Medicine. She is specialized in health promotion, wellbeing, doctor-patience interaction, health care, identity, gender, and violence.

Sara Patrizia Desole is founder and president of the "Prospettiva Donna Association". Second level Master's degree in European Politics, obtained at the University of London (Birkbeck College), with a thesis on *Theories of Ethnic conflicts: a Test of a Model*. Trainer, she is member of the Gender Violence Table of the Autonomous Region of Sardinia. Collaborates with the University Center for Gender Studies A.R.G.IN.O. of the University of Sassari.

Angela Di Stasi Full Professor of European Union Law and International Law, Department of Legal Sciences- University of Salerno. Rector's Delegate for equal opportunities. Director of the Ph.D School in Legal Sciences. Director of the

"Observatory on the Area of Freedom, Security and Justice" and Director of the online scientific review "Freedom, Security & Justice: European Legal Studies".

Gaudi Simona, PhD. She is a Researcher at the Italian National Institute of Health (Istituto Superiore di Sanità, ISS). After a degree in Biological Sciences, she obtained the PhD in Biotechnology at UCDavis, Usa and University of Milan, Italy. Principal Investigator at IARC (International Agency Research on Cancer), she focussed her research in Genetics of Cancer. Since 2002, she is a permanent staff at ISS. From 2004 her research project is the implication of the implicit genome as genetic determinants in complex diseases. In 2015 she joined the Department of Environment and Health for studying the epigenetic profile of women that experienced Intimate Partner Violence.

Paola Giannoni, Ph.D. and Doctor Europaeus in Sociology, is currently Postdoctoral Research Fellow at the University of Genova, Italy. Her main topics are related to social inequality, with a specific focus on ageism and social inclusion of older people.

Anna Iermano Assistant Professor of International Law, Department of Legal Sciences, University of Salerno. Professor of "International and Procedural Private Law", Department of Legal Sciences. Member of the "Observatory on the Area of Freedom, Security and Justice" and of the Editorial Board of the online Review "Freedom, Security and Justice: European Legal Studies".

Giuseppe Masullo is an Associate Professor of General Sociology and directs International Lab for innovative social research (ILIS), laboratory of interdisciplinary studies and research that promote theoretical, epistemological and methodological advances in the field of social sciences through constant dialogue with scholars who are experts in both national and international. His interests, in the methodological field, focus on the area of digital methods applied to the study of disadvantaged and discriminated categories due to their gender and sexual identity.

Sara Mellano is a psychologist and psychotherapy trainee, interning at a support service for gender-based violence survivors under ASL Roma 2. She is also a researcher at the Italian National Institute of Health (ISS), collaborating on the project "Violence Against Women: Long-term Health Effects for Precision Prevention.

Giada Moretti is Ph.D. student at the University of Genova, Italy. Hermain topics are active ageing and social inclusion of older people.

Assunta Penna is PhD in Social theory, digital innovation and public policies. She has participated in international and national conferences and published papers in scholarly journals (Media Education, Comunicación y Género, Central European Political Science Review) and in volume (Mimesis, Springer, Pàtron, Franco Angeli). Her main research interests include media languages, the digitalization of public institutions, Internet studies and gender studies.

Maria Lucia Piga PhD in the University of Pisa, since 2001 is Associate Professor at the University of Sassari (Department of Humanities and Social Sciences), in which she teaches Sociology. In the same University she is founder (2018) and director of the Interdisciplinary Center for gender studies A.R.G.IN.O. – Advanced Research on Gender INequalities and Opportunities. From 2018 is membership in the scientific committee of AIS – Gender Studies.

Debora Maria Pizzimenti holds a PhD in Cognitive Sciences. She is an expert in the field of "Cultural Industries and Media Studies" and a researcher at the University of Messina. She is the author of several articles published in journals such as Metis and Media Education – Studies, Research, and Good Practices, CORISCO editions, and has presented her findings at national and international conferences.

Stefano Poli, Ph.D, is full professor in Sociology at the University of Genova, Italy. His main topics are related to social inequality, with a specific focus on health and ageing.

Barbara Segatto is an Associate Professor at the Department of Political Science, Law and International Studies at the University of Padova where she teaches Sociology of Families and Childhood and Social Services at the Degree Course in Social Work. Her main research topics concern social work practices with children and their families with a particular focus on child protection, adoptive and foster families.

Maria Concetta Segneri, MA, medical anthropologist. She has been working at the Italian National Institute for Health, Migration and Poverty since 2008. Applied field: biomedical and psychological clinical support, training of social and health workers, qualitative research. Topics: gender-based violence; forced migration; modelling of health interventions for breaking down access barriers, improving health risk assessment, health education on specific topics.

Sonia Viale, psychologist, works at the National Institute for Migration, Health and Poverty. Has acquired advanced competences in the recognition and treatment of issues related to gender violence, Community awareness raising and training of health and social workers. Project manager with the Ministry of Health, lecturer and trainer in conferences, seminars, congresses, training courses and university masters, scientific director of courses, author and co-author of articles on gender justice and migration.

Baltische Studien zur Erziehungs- und Sozialwissenschaft /
Baltic Studies in Educational and Social Sciences

Herausgegeben von / Edited by Gerd-Bodo von Carlsburg,
Natalija Mažeikienė & Airi Liimets

Band 17   Gerd-Bodo von Carlsburg (Hrsg./ed.): Qualität von Bildung und Kultur. Theorie und Praxis. The Quality of Education and Culture. Theoretical and Practical Dimensions. 2009.

Band 18   Airi Liimets (Hrsg.): Denkkulturen. Selbstwerdung des Menschen. Erziehungskulturen. Festschrift für Professor Dr. Dr. h.c. Dr. h.c. Heino Liimets. 2010.

Band 19   Ellu Saar (ed.): Towards a Normal Stratification Order. Actual and Perceived Social Stratification in Post-Socialist Estonia. 2011.

Band 20   Marika Veisson / Eeva Hujala / Peter K. Smith/ Manjula Waniganayake / Eve Kikas (eds.): Global Perspectives in Early Childhood Education. Diversity, Challenges and Possibilities. 2011.

Band 21   Airi Liimets / Marit Mäesalu (eds.): Music Inside and Outside the School. 2011

Band 22   Gerd-Bodo von Carlsburg (Hrsg./ed.): Enkulturation durch sozialen Kompetenzerwerb. Enculturation by Acquiring of Social Competences. 2011.

Band 23   Reet Liimets: Ich als raumzeitliches Konstrukt. Die Fiktionen vom Leben der estnischen und deutschen Jugendlichen. 2012.

Band 24   Raivo Vetik (ed.): Nation-Building in the Context of Post-Communist Transformation and Globalization. The Case of Estonia. 2012.

Band 25   Airi-Alina Allaste (ed.): ‚Back in the West'. Changing Lifestyles in Transforming Societies. 2013.

Band 26   Gerd-Bodo von Carlsburg (Hrsg./ed.): Bildungswissenschaft auf der Suche nach globaler Identität. Educational Sciences in Search of Global Identity. 2013.

Band 27   Airi Liimets / Marika Veisson (eds): Teachers and Youth in Educational Reality. 2014.

Band 28   Gerd-Bodo von Carlsburg / Thomas Vogel (Hrsg./eds.): Bildungswissenschaften und akademisches Selbstverständnis in einer globalisierten Welt. Education and Academic Self-Concept in the Globalized World. 2014.

Band 29   Marika Veisson / Airi Liimets / Pertti Kansanen / Edgar Krull (eds.): Tradition and Innovation in Education. 2015.

Band 30   Robertas Jucevičius / Jurgita Bruneckienė / Gerd-Bodo von Carlsburg (eds.): International Practices of Smart Development. 2015.

Band 31   Gerd-Bodo von Carlsburg (Hrsg./ed.): Strategien der Lehrerbildung. Zur Steigerung von Lehrkompetenzen und Unterrichtsqualität. Strategies for Teacher Training. Concepts for Improving Skills and Quality of Teaching. 2016.

Band 32   Gerd-Bodo von Carlsburg (Hrsg./ed.): Denk- und Lernkulturen im wissenschaftlichen Diskurs. Cultures of Thinking and Learning in the Scientific Discourse. 2017.

Band 33   Palmira Pečiuliauskienė / Aleksa Valdemaras: Motivation of New Generation Students for Learning Physics and Mathematics. 2018.

Band 34   Gerd-Bodo von Carlsburg (Hrsg./ed.): Transkulturelle Perspektiven in der Bildung. Transcultural Perspectives in Education. 2019.

**Neue Denkansätze in den Bildungs- und Sozialwissenschaften /
New Approaches in Educational and Social Sciences**

Herausgegeben von / Edited by Gerd-Bodo von Carlsburg,
Anne Kirschner & Natalija Mažeikienė

www.peterlang.com